Jodie
FOSTER

Jodie
FOSTER
A Life on Screen

PHILIPPA KENNEDY

A BIRCH LANE PRESS BOOK
Published by Carol Publishing Group

First Carol Publishing Group edition 1996

A Birch Lane Press Book
Published by Carol Publishing Group
Birch Lane Press is a registered trademark of Carol Communications,
    Inc.
Editorial Offices: 600 Madison Avenue, New York, N.Y. 10022
Sales & Distribution Offices: 120 Enterprise Avenue, Secaucus,
    N.J. 07094
In Canada: Canadian Manda Group, One Atlantic Avenue, Suite 105,
    Toronto, Ontario M6K 3E7

Queries regarding rights and permissions should be addressed to
Carol Publishing Group, 600 Madison Avenue, New York, N.Y. 10022

Carol Publishing Group books are available at special discounts for
bulk purchases, sales promotions, fund-raising, or educational
purposes. Special editions can be created to specifications. For
details contact: Special Sales Department, Carol Publishing
Group, 120 Enterprise Avenue, Secaucus, N.J. 07094

First published in Great Britain in 1995 by Macmillan London Ltd

Manufactured in the United States of America
10   9   8   7   6   5   4   3   2   1

Library of Congress Cataloging-in-Publication Data

Kennedy, Philippa
    Jodie Foster : a life on screen / Philippa Kennedy.
        p.   cm.
    "A Birch Lane Press book."
    ISBN 1-55972-348-3 (hardcover)
    1. Foster, Jodie.   2. Motion picture actors and actresses—United
States—Biography.   3. Motion picture producers and directors—
United States—Biography.   I. Title.
PN2287.F624K46   1996
791.43'028'092—dc20
    [B]   95-47833
                                                                  CIP

CONTENTS

PICTURE ACKNOWLEDGMENTS

The author and publisher wish to acknowledge the following, with grateful thanks, for permission to include photographs in the plate section of this book:

ALPHA: Page 6, *bottom right*; page 8, *top right, and bottom left and right.*

ASSOCIATED PRESS LTD: Page 5, *bottom left and right.*

LONDON FEATURES: Page 5, *middle*; page 6, *bottom left*; page 7, *top right, and bottom left and right.*

REX FEATURES: Page 2, *top left, and bottom left*; page 3, *bottom right*; page 7, *top left.*

RONALD GRANT: Page 1, *top, middle, and bottom left*; page 2, *top right*; page 3, *top and bottom left*; page 5, *top*; page 6, *top left.*

SCOPE FEATURES: Page 4, *bottom*; page 6, *top right.*

SYGMA: Page 1, *bottom right.*

UNIVERSAL PICTORIAL PRESS AGENCY LTD: Page 8, *top left.*

Every effort has been made to trace all copyright holders but if any have been inadvertently overlooked, the author and publishers will be pleased to make the necessary arrangement at the first opportunity.

ACKNOWLEDGMENTS

I would like to thank all those people who gave me practical help and encouragement in writing this book, starting with Alan Frame who suggested it, literary agent Judith Chilcote who had the confidence to make me do it, my editors at Macmillan, Peta Nightingale and Jane Wood, who nursed me through it, and *Daily Express* Editor Sir Nicholas Lloyd for his permission to do it. Thanks to my husband John for building me a study to write it in and for his endless support and, for their invaluable help with research, thanks to Pam Parker, Lucy Broadbent, Robyn Foyster, Lesley O'Toole, Louise Gannon, Jill Evans, Charles Fawcett, John Hiscock, Gary Jenkins, Patrick Pachecho, Douglas Thomson, the Dudley Freeman Library in New York, Desmond Wilcox, John Hinckley's lawyer Vincent J. Fuller and his secretary Mary Caton, Martin Dunn for the use of the *New York Daily News* library, Yvon Samuel in Paris, Anne Cooper of Chiswick Library, Stuart White, Billy McDonald, Randall Widner, Mike Walker, Paul Harris, Nicola Parfitt.

Other journalists who have interviewed Jodie Foster over the years and whose articles formed a valuable part of my research must also be acknowledged including those whose work has been published in *People* magazine and *Vanity Fair*.

Finally a special thanks to Jane Woods for doing the picture research.

INTRODUCTION

In downtown Los Angeles, March 1988, the crowds outside the Dorothy Chandler Pavilion had been gathering since dawn, anxious for a place on the pavements as near as possible to their idols on the most important day of Hollywood's calendar . . . the Oscars ceremony.

From early morning the Los Angeles Police Department were putting up barricades and cordoning off streets. With billions of dollars' worth of movie stardom arriving in just a few hours' time they were taking no risks with security. By midday the sniffer dogs used by the bomb squad had done their job around the six-hundred-seat auditorium and plain clothes detectives scanned the faces of the fans for the one star-crazed lunatic who might want to claim his fifteen minutes of fame.

They were only too aware that one of the nominees for best actress, Jodie Foster, had already inspired two such 'crazies'. John Hinckley is still in a secure mental hospital after his attempt, in 1981, to assassinate President Reagan to impress Jodie. And Edward Richardson, who shared Hinckley's obsession, served three months for illegal possession of a firearm with intent.

Miles away in the unfashionable San Fernando Valley, north of Los Angeles, Jodie was breakfasting as usual on fresh fruit and herb tea, trying not to think too much about the Oscars. If the shadow of Hinckley flitted through her mind at all, it was quickly banished. The subject is now a closed book, not to be picked over and dwelt on. She said what she had to say about it shortly after it happened, and has steadfastly refused to discuss it ever since.

It is one of two subjects which are off limits. The other is her personal life. Whom she may or may not have slept with is strictly taboo. It is also what makes her so fascinating.

That warm March night in 1988 when her diminutive figure

stepped out of the huge stretch limo with its darkened windows, it was clear that she was a favourite of the crowd. After all, they have known her since she was a little girl doing ads for suntan lotion and dog food. The cheer that went up was warm and appreciative, and the smile on Jodie's face acknowledged her pleasure.

Her choice of dress was something of a statement itself – strapless blue, mini-skirted with a train, at a time when few women wore 'short' on such a grand occasion. Her hair was simply washed and allowed to flop naturally around her pretty face. The message was, 'I'm young, this is me, so what the heck?'

Yet Jodie, a child of Tinseltown, was nothing if not respectful and as always had something to say. The previous year's best actor, Michael Douglas, presented her with an Oscar for best actress for her role as a rape victim in *The Accused*. As she joyfully accepted it, she used the opportunity to express strongly although never stridently held feminist beliefs. 'For too long women have been portrayed as the second sex. I want to make a movie about that, about my generation and sexuality. It's about time people had frank movies where sexuality is treated really honestly, where women are sexual people instead of constantly being on some non-sexual pedestal,' she said. She has yet to make that movie but you can be sure she will, in her own time and when she finds the perfect script.

Jodie Foster has carved out a special position for herself in Hollywood. At the age of thirty-two she has the same number of films to her name. She has won Oscars for two of them and directed one herself, starring in it as well. Right now she is one of the most powerful and marketable women in the movie world, but still she remains an enigma.

She eschews the life of a Tinseltown big-shot, preferring to live simply in a rented apartment in West Hollywood not far from her offices. She also has her small house in Woodland Hills in the San Fernando Valley, miles away from the starry mansions of Bel Air and Beverly Hills which she visits every so often. She loves the anonymity of suburbia and enjoys dropping her own clothes into the dry-cleaners and browsing through the current crop of videos at a shopping arcade just like anyone else.

It is, perhaps, a very conscious attempt to live what she sees as a normal life in the very abnormal world of movie-making which she inhabits. Away from a film set she is almost obsessive about not standing out from the crowd and determined to go about her everyday life unrestricted by her fame. She says herself that the only place she feels safe is on a film set, and it's not just because she is protected by security guards. It's the one place she can drop the cool and collected front she shows to the world and plumb the depths of her emotions surrounded by people who understand.

Few people are allowed to witness that in real life. She doesn't let many people close enough. The most important relationship in her life to date is with her mother Brandy, who divorced her father, Lucius Foster, before Jodie was born. It was Brandy who taught her daughter that she could do and be anything she wanted to.

Jodie paid tribute to the strength of that relationship when she accepted that first Oscar in a speech that has become legendary in Hollywood. She said: 'This is such a big deal and my life is so simple. There are very few things – there's love and work and family.

'And this movie is so special to us because it was all three of those things. And I'd like to thank all of my families, the tribes that I come from, the wonderful crew on *The Accused*, Jonathan Kaplan, Kelly McGillis, Tom Topor, Paramount, the Academy, my schools . . . and most importantly my mother, Brandy, who taught me that all my finger paintings were Picassos and that I didn't have to be afraid.

'And mostly that cruelty might be very human and it might be very cultural but it's not acceptable, which is what this movie is all about. Thank you so much.'

That speech neatly and eloquently encapsulated Jodie's code for life. She is and always has been her own person. She lives her life in a straightforward and uncompromising way, with apologies to nobody and concern for everybody.

When she was just thirteen, she made an extraordinarily accurate prediction to one startled interviewer: 'Of course, maybe when I get through with this town they'll have something to write.'

They already do and she's not even halfway through.

ONE

Brandy Foster – Stage Mother

Hollywood has always been a magnet for ambitious parents. Behind every child star there is a pushy mother doing the rounds of agents and producers, hoping her pretty daughter will be the next Shirley Temple. Only a few ever do make it. The ones who graduate through to adulthood can practically be counted on the fingers of one hand. Mickey Rooney, Judy Garland, Natalie Wood and Hayley Mills were the biggest names, but none came close to wielding the kind of influence that Jodie Foster does.

Garland never found the stability and love she craved. Her childhood years were spent making films and she kept herself going on pills to wake her up and more pills to make her sleep. Later there were alcohol and stronger drugs. Judy didn't have a mother like Brandy Foster to look after her. Jodie, however, did, and Brandy has been the single most enduring influence on her life. It has, on the whole, been a thoroughly good and rewarding influence and something that Jodie is very conscious of.

When Jodie paid her moving tribute to her mother at the Oscars, Brandy was in tears. Although she was the guiding hand, she knew Jodie was and always has been her own person; nevertheless she was touched by the public acknowledgement. Even today, at the age of thirty-two, Jodie will dismiss any talk of 'stage mothers'. She knows what her mother went through to give her a lasting and successful career, the sacrifices she made and the encouragement she gave.

Brandy was born in the Bronx and given the name of Evelyn,

which she disliked. Nicknamed Brandy after a childhood tippling incident, in her teens she decided to abandon 'Evelyn' altogether. She was brought up in Rockford, Illinois, but made up her mind at an early age that she would leave small-town America behind her just as soon as she was able.

After she finished high school – St Mary's Academy in Milwaukee – she and a girlfriend, Gloria Cannon, pooled their resources and set out to drive to Los Angeles. In the fifties LA seemed the most glamorous place in the world and Brandy wanted a piece of it. In those days she was a blue-eyed blonde, pretty and vivacious but too shy to have a go at stardom herself. She got herself a job as a buyer of baby clothes for Robinson's Department Store.

Before long she met and fell in love with a dashing Air Force Officer from a wealthy Chicago family – Lucius Foster – and they were married in Las Vegas in 1953, Brandy for the first time, Lucius for the second. Brandy was far too much in love to have reservations about a man who did not appear to have much contact with his three sons by his first marriage. It did not ring any alarm bells with her that he made little attempt to see them, a pattern that was to be repeated when Lucius left Brandy.

But at first the marriage was a happy one and Brandy bore four children – Lucinda, born in 1954, Constance in 1955, and in 1957 came Lucius IV, nicknamed Buddy; Alicia Christian was born on 19 November 1962 and immediately Brandy started to call her Jodie simply because she had gone off the name Alicia and liked Jodie better. Jodie was grateful for this in later years. Just like her mother, she hated the names she was christened. She said: 'Those are the names the family wanted, but when my mother got me home from the hospital she hated them so she always called me Jodie. If anyone called me by those names now to aggravate me, I'd hit 'em.'

By the time Jodie arrived, Brandy had also gone off her husband Lucius. In fact, although the marriage lasted officially for ten years, through the latter years it was struggling. On the morning Brandy appeared in the divorce court she was pregnant with Jodie, although she didn't know it. With her marriage over and three children to support, the last thing Brandy needed was another child. Yet as the baby grew inside her a special bond was formed between them. Many women would have cracked under the strain but Brandy was made of sterner stuff. She determined that she and her young family would survive.

By this stage the gregarious Brandy, who worked part-time as a press agent, had a large circle of women friends – the word 'networking' might have been conceived especially for her. One friend, Josephine Hill, came to the rescue, inviting her and her three and a half children to move into her large house. Brandy set about working out how they were going to earn enough to feed and clothe them all and pay the rent.

There was no question of sitting back and watching the alimony accumulate in her bank account. Even though the law in California allows a wife half of everything, the couple had very little in the form of assets. Brandy was awarded $600 a month and for the first three or four months the money came in. To start with it was paid into her bank account late, and then, possibly because of Lucius's own financial problems, it became rather spasmodic.

Brandy remembers: 'Then I found myself running up and down to his real estate office, pleading for the support money. "I have to have this. I have to have that." As any divorced wife knows, it's a very humiliating position, like a dog begging for a bone. I would have to create a big scene, stage a tantrum. Then I would be given enough to tide me over just for that period.'

Lucius appeared simply to close his mind to his second young family. He seems to have made little attempt to keep in touch, and the children would barely recognize him if they happened to meet in the street. As always there are two sides to any story, and Lucius says now that it was the way Brandy wanted it. The bitterness was so fierce that he felt it was better for everybody if he stayed away. One way or another he had no stomach for a fight. Lucius likes a smooth life. He hates rows. It was easier just to cut himself off from his family.

By the time she was in her teens Jodie had met her father just four times. She insists that it was never a problem. So many of her friends' parents were divorced that it seemed quite normal to a child growing up in Hollywood. If she secretly missed having a father, she kept it to herself. Being part of a one-parent family gave her a kind of strength which was reinforced by her admiration for and fierce loyalty to her mother.

She was adept at fielding questions about it, often dismissively, but when she was twenty-eight Jodie talked about it candidly. 'I am a little obsessed by the theme of the one-parent family because it is the only thing that I know. And all the kids with whom I grew up were in the same boat. My mother's friends were divorced women. I heard them talking for hours on end about "that bastard" – the men came and went but the women stayed.

'There was Aunt this and Aunt that and they'd pick me up from school and she'd pick up their kids. It was like you had a new family – the non-nuclear American family. The casualities of divorce. It wasn't horrible. It was just – what it was.'

Many of these women friends were bitter. Few, Brandy included, had anything good to say about their 'exes', although in retrospect leaving her was probably the best thing Lucius ever did for her. Jodie's life might have been very different if the need to earn a living had not been there when she was so young.

One of Josephine Hill's neighbours had an eight-year-old son who played with Buddy. The boy was already making television commercials and Buddy begged to be allowed to do the same. It was just what Brandy needed – something that would bring in the housekeeping money without her leaving the children. She began trawling the agencies with all the other hopeful mothers. After drawing one or two blanks, the women's networking system came up with a woman who was building up a good reputation as a successful agent, working from home out of her garage. That didn't bother Brandy. She recognized a kindred spirit in Toni Kelman, and she was right.

Toni took one look at the blond, blue-eyed all-American boy and pronounced him 'perfect'. The first three advertising agencies who interviewed him hired him. He did ads for Kellogg's Cereals,

Mattel Toys and a pet food brand, earning $110 per job. The Fosters were on their way.

Brandy was able to move the family out of her friend's house and into a rented home in Newport Beach down the coast, but as Buddy's career blossomed this became impractical. It was too far from the work they needed and Brandy decided that, even though it was cheaper to live in Newport Beach, she needed to find somewhere in Hollywood. She was also developing her own work as a film publicist for producer Arthur Jacobs.

Eventually she found a small villa in a run-down area of town. It was shabby and ramshackle, but Brandy had taste and turned it into a stylish and interesting home. She had it painted a warm terracotta to give it an Italian feel. Jodie has fond memories of her childhood there. 'We didn't have much, but what we had was exquisite. Like, we always had good Tuscan bread around and my mother drove a Peugeot and she took us to arty movies. We were a cool, cultured family.'

Brandy dabbled in antiques and was always buying and selling elegant chairs which found a home in their villa for a short time before being sold. Said Jodie: 'My mother collects chairs. Hundreds of chairs. And everything she's bought has gone up incredibly in value. So every time we became poor – because we were rich, then poor, rich, then poor – she'd just sell the chairs.' There was never enough surplus cash to save much but even as a child Jodie tried to squirrel away a few pennies when she could.

Brandy instilled in her children an appreciation of the finer things in life, like her antique chairs, even when they couldn't afford them. Said Jodie: 'We had beautiful furniture and leather-bound books in different languages. My mum is a real Francophile – she read French books and magazines and she sent me to the Lycée. As a family we went to museums and movies and Mum put a premium, a real emphasis, on curiosity. She gave us all an aesthetic sense that has nothing to do with making money. There is a kind of American complacency in this town that I never became part of.

'We'd do movies – then we'd just spend it all. The best line in *The Hotel New Hampshire*, that really says it all about the craziness that goes on in the family, is: "We're eccentric and we're bizarre, but to each other we're just our family." That's pretty much the truth. The weirdest things happened in my family, but they probably happen in every family. You just take it with a grain of salt.'

When Jodie was a toddler her brother Buddy was the family breadwinner, earning about $25,000 a year. But Brandy was advised that he was becoming over-exposed in commercials and should start doing proper acting parts in television shows. A series called *Green Acres* was the first, followed by *Hondo*, and then came *Mayberry RFD*, which kept him working for four years. The two older girls, Lucinda and Connie, were doing well at local schools but neither showed any inclination to go into the movies, although they appeared in one or two commericals initially. Brandy did not try to force them – they were naturally more reserved than their brother. But Jodie was different.

Said Brandy: 'She's always been a gifted child. I recognized that early in her life. She started to talk when she was nine months old. She taught herself to read when she was three. One day we were driving along and she began reading billboard signs aloud to me. I thought she had memorized what her older sister had taught her. I soon found out, much to my amazement, that she could read. I know it sounds incredible, but when Jodie was five she could pick up a script and read it cold.'

Jodie's brother Buddy has an explanation for her early development. 'We didn't have a father so Connie, Lucinda and I became fathers to Jodie when she was little. We talked to her the whole time, showing her things. We taught her to read when she was two years old.'

She was a delightful little girl, always smiling, always funny. Adults were charmed by her, especially her mother. 'She's always had a great sense of humour. She once picked up a ratty old fur coat from a trash barrel and just walked down the street in it. She has always been allowed to dress the way she wanted to,' said Brandy. Even then she was a child who knew her own mind. She was never interested in girls' toys like Barbie and Ken. Her most cherished possession was a model of Babar, the elephant that spoke French.

The family was still in Newport Beach when the three-year-old Jodie charmed her way into the business. Buddy, who was then eight, was auditioning for a Coppertone ad and Brandy had driven him up to Hollywood with Jodie in the car. She couldn't leave her in the car alone so Brandy took her in with them, and the pretty blonde child enchanted the Coppertone executives. She got the job. Buddy didn't.

Buddy remembers the day well: 'She was just "live" all the time. She would walk through the door and everyone was just enchanted. The Coppertone interview was for me. They told me to take my shirt off and saw that I had freckles all over my body. Suddenly I noticed they were all laughing and there behind me was little Jodie flexing her muscles. They asked her who she was and she answers, "I'm Alexander the Great." They just loved her. We had been teaching her things since she could just about open her eyes, and the Alexander the Great thing just popped out.'

Soon the cute toddler was as much in demand as her brother, and the family had two wages coming into the house. But Brandy wisely remembered the advice she had been given about her son and when Jodie reached the age of eight she stopped her doing any more commercials. Her own work as a press agent was invaluable when it came to guiding her two children through the jungle of the Hollywood television world, and she was sensible enough to listen to advice yet trust her own instincts.

'I got a lot of static from the agents. They thought I was crazy,' she said.

Crazy or not, she stuck by her decision and furthermore demanded twice as much for Jodie as other children were being paid. In those days the rate was $420 a week. Brandy asked for $1000 and got it. Jodie did ads for biscuits and pet food, and later she landed a role in *Mayberry RFD* along with her brother. She was also picked for parts in top-rated series like *Gunsmoke*, *Bonanza* and *The Partridge Family*.

Years later she remembers those years of doing television ads as hours and hours of eating disgusting things and having her hair washed. 'I remember being in commercials and doing them over and over again, having to eat sickening things all day and throwing up. After being in a shampoo ad I couldn't get the shit out of my hair for ten days. But there were people on those sets and on movie sets who were like my family – a misfit family of people who did not lead conventional lives. They played with me, but they also reprimanded me when I got bratty.'

At that stage Jodie never knew what she would be doing next. As far as regular work was concerned, the nearest she got was when Paramount signed her up for the *Paper Moon* series based on the hit movie starring Ryan O'Neal and his precocious daughter Tatum. Scheduled against the top-rated family show *The Waltons*, it failed, and Brandy decided that from then on it would be feature films only. Jodie was too good to be wasted on television.

Jack Shea, who directed her in *Paper Moon*, recalls her as a 'delightful little girl'. He said: 'Jodie was always considered such a little professional. She actually seemed to understand what she was doing and liked it. I never felt sorry for her, unlike some of the other kids I worked with where you could always tell they were just counting the minutes till they could go home.'

Throughout those years Brandy was selfless. There was no time for other men and anyway, as she said herself: 'Do you know any man in his right mind who would want to come into this house and take on the responsibility of four children with all the sibling rivalries going on?' She had the support of her circle of women friends, many of whom were also struggling to raise children without the support of husbands.

Brandy was always strict but fair, kind but insistent that they said 'please' and 'thank you', helped with the household chores and avoided becoming the spoilt 'Hollywood brats' that they might have become without a firm hand guiding them. The children were never allowed to come and go as they pleased. Jodie didn't have a house key until she was much older. Her mother was always there for her.

'She taught me tact, diplomacy and politeness. She taught me to send thank you notes,' said Jodie. They were a close family unit and Brandy was quick to instil in her children feelings of responsibility for the welfare of the others. Said Jodie: 'All of us were in it together. My sisters took care of the house, my brother did commercials and TV, I took care of the trash and concentrated on my studies. My mom worked, we all did. Just to survive.' Speaking from an adult viewpoint Jodie is typically modest about her contribution and always careful to emphasize the roles of her brother and sisters.

Brandy admits she was a strict mother. 'I've had to be. Lots of times I'd have liked to have been softer. But all four of my children were just waiting for me to break down. They would have taken advantage.' As with any other teenager there were times when Jodie would do anything to wriggle out of household chores, but Brandy never let her get away with it. At the time she said:

'She's an ordinary child. Off the set the things she does – even the things she doesn't do, like not doing her share of the chores in the house – are exactly the things you would expect from any teenager. As well as being her mother I am also her number-one fan. Jodie is just a very, very nice person to be with. She really is very good company indeed. She's witty and generous and imaginative. Just watching her and being with her is fascinating.'

There were trips to the theatre and the cinema and take-away Chinese meals. Always there were films to watch and discuss. Jodie spent hours in darkened cinemas with her mother while her friends were out in the California sunshine getting brown. She was fascinated by the movies. They were the world she wanted to be in, and she wanted to understand everything about them.

Brandy would also talk to her daughter about world events, politics, civil rights and injustice. She would take her to civil rights rallies and marches and discuss their implications. If she was watching television she was taught not just to sit there mindlessly, but to form opinions, be critical. When she was eleven Jodie's opinions were strong and forcefully expressed. *MASH* was her favourite, but a show called *All in the Family* was scorned 'because they seemed to be doing the same thing each week'. She liked *Kung Fu* to begin with because it started off as a peace show, but it was soon switched off as it became more violent. 'I think violence on TV is bad for kids,' she pronounced solemnly. She fell asleep during the controversial *Last Tango in Paris*, starring Marlon Brando and Maria Schneider, with its notorious sex scene in an empty apartment. But she wouldn't bother to watch her own *Paper Moon* because she didn't much care for country shows.

Jodie was never told to keep her opinions to herself and nobody ever 'talked her down' or told her to keep quiet during an argument. Brandy listened attentively to everything she said. More important, Brandy taught her that she was capable of doing anything she wanted in her life – nothing was beyond her in a world which was beginning to recognize that sexual equality was here to stay.

Jodie recalls: 'I remember sitting under a lemon tree outside my house when I was five or six when my mom came out and said: "You know, you are just so lucky to be a woman now because you can do anything you want to do." The message, I realized even then, was that she couldn't and that I was going to be different.'

It was by no means force-fed feminism. Jodie was receptive but Brandy allowed all her children to be just that as well . . . children. There was plenty of laughter and silliness in the young household.

It may have been an unusual upbringing, but it gave Jodie a special confidence in herself and her own opinions and an ability to express them. She said: 'You feel more confident if you've been continually asked questions like "What kind of wine do you think we should have?" or "What do you think of Richard Nixon?" or whatever. Now I know that, in a way, it was a ruse to make me feel I had control of my life and that ultimately, if I had said, "I want to do this porno movie" or something and my Mom didn't agree, she would have said, "No way!"

'But I also realize that a lot of the decisions she made were, in some ways, vicarious decisions. My mother didn't want me to make lots of money and go on to have a flash-in-the-pan career. She didn't want me to make hoopla comedies where I would wear cute pigtails and tutus. She wanted me to be taken seriously and to be a moral person and looked up to as somebody who stood for the right things.

'And when I did *Taxi Driver*, it's not as if she didn't know who Martin Scorsese was – she dragged me to see *Mean Streets* four times. It's not like she said, "Oh, a movie about a prostitute. I think I'll put my little girl in that." She was very aware of Scorsese as a talent.'

While Connie and Lucinda got on with their studies, Buddy and Jodie combined theirs with the task of earning the family living. They did nothing without their mother's approval. Producers knew that if they wanted the children they had to get past Brandy and all scripts were sent to her.

As Buddy grew into his teens and his cuteness faded, his television work began to wane. Jodie's, however, flourished, as much for her looks as for her professional attitude and ability to learn her lines quickly. In fact that hardly stretched her at all. Brandy knew she was an exceptional child and needed added stimulation that the local high school was never going to provide. With a modest but solid income from her film work in the bank, the fashionable Lycée Français, run by Madame Esther Kabbaz, was within their reach and Brandy felt it would expand the eight-year-old Jodie's already fertile and enquiring mind. It also turned her into a fluent French speaker, which enabled her to do films in France without having her voice dubbed. The Lycée was considered to be one of the best schools in Los Angeles, and many children of famous parents were sent there.

In Brandy's eyes all things European were romantic and exciting, very much worth adopting. She accepted several jobs for Jodie which were to take them both to Europe to make and promote films, and Jodie found Paris an enchanting city. She enjoyed showing off her fluency. It gave her incredible self-confidence to be able to hold press conferences in French, and endeared her to a nation not always willing to embrace those who were not French-speakers.

When Jodie was twelve, Brandy met a man whom she liked well enough to consider marrying. There had been the occasional date with other men, but Dr Jacques Gabay, a cardiologist who practised in Nice, sparked off something in Brandy that she had thought she would never feel again. She was introduced by Madame Kabbaz, Jodie's headmistress, who had become a friend. In an interview, Brandy enthused about the doctor: 'It was just like electricity. We sort of sparked and we've been seeing each other intermittently ever since. And I must say it has been a welcome change.'

Brandy liked him enough to invite him to Los Angeles for Connie's wedding, a glitzy affair with several showbusiness stars as guests. The family encouraged the romance. Connie said: 'Mother has sacrificed herself for all of us, and frankly we'd like for her to make a new life for herself. She's still a relatively young, attractive woman in her forties and there's no reason why she shouldn't get married again or become a management executive.'

But the romance fizzled out and Dr Gabay, now nearly eighty but still teaching cardiology in Nice, says it was never a serious affair. 'I am not going to discuss my private life because I am a gentleman, but I never had any intention of marrying. It was not like that at all. I was closer to the child, Jodie. She impressed me with her intelligence. I would give her advice and she would listen like an adult even though she was only twelve.'

There were other boyfriends, but none of the romances ever came to anything. They all took second place to managing Jodie's career and few men will put up with that. Said Buddy: 'When I was about ten she had met this man and they were going to get married, but it fizzled out. I wanted my mom to marry someone. I wanted a dad but it never happened. She hated my father and she hated men full stop.'

Buddy's memories are certainly vivid, but clearly coloured by his own personal pain. However, Brandy never remarried. She became Jodie's official manager, set up a trust fund, paid herself a salary, and got to work. 'I approached it as a real business. I felt that was the way to do it. I've tried to build Jodie's career, although sometimes I didn't know if I was making the right decisions,' she said.

She was always on the look-out for something unusual for her daughter. It was important that Jodie did not become type-cast as the gutsy young tomboy she played so well, although Brandy rejected one agent's advice to put her in a dress and have her hair curled. If she knew one thing about her daughter it was that she would never have been comfortable trying to be the reincarnation of Shirley Temple. Said Jodie: 'She'd seen a lot of wayward souls in Hollywood. She didn't want a cripple for a child. She wanted me to fly. She also wanted me to have a serious and heroic career. So she chose some risky, off-beat movies.'

Producers who wanted Jodie would submit their scripts for Brandy to read first. Dozens would arrive each week, to be stacked in an alcove in the stairs at the villa not far from the Hollywood Bowl. After Brandy had made her selection Jodie would have the final say: 'If I don't happen to like a director or if I don't care for the script, I'll turn down a role.'

When Jodie did an interview Brandy was generally there, watching, listening, directing, always vigilant, always aware of how her daughter was coming across. If Jodie put her feet up on a dressing table, for example, Brandy would bark at her: 'Don't do that, Jodie.' She would chip in with the occasional answer and never tried of singing her daughter's praises. Journalists inevitably described her as 'shrewd' or 'calculating' or 'pushy'.

Between the ages of eleven and thirteen Jodie appeared in some wildly different films, from *Alice Doesn't Live Here Any More*, in which she played a street-wise urchin, to the gangster's moll Tallulah in the 1920s' gangster spoof *Bugsy Malone*. Then there was *The Little Girl Who Lives Down the Lane*, in which Jodie was a psychotic killer.

All the time Brandy travelled with Jodie, helping her learn her lines, doing her laundry, making sure she ate properly and protecting her from the dangers and temptations of the heady world she lived in. Her vigilance was rewarded by a well-adjusted and poised daughter well able to handle the disappointments without resorting to the 'shrinks' favoured by so many young actors, or, worse still, drugs.

But there were times when others felt Brandy pushed too hard. Allowing her thirteen-year-old daughter to play the part of a child prostitute in *Taxi Driver* was one. The idea scandalized the nation, and Brandy was roundly condemned for exposing the adolescent Jodie to the seamier side of life, which many people felt she was too young to handle.

Martin Scorsese, who directed Jodie as the street urchin in *Alice Doesn't Live Here Any More*, was convinced she would be perfect as the scantily clad street-walker Iris opposite Robert de Niro, and Brandy knew it was a part that would make Jodie's career and allow her to graduate naturally from cheeky tomboy to grown-up actress. She also knew her daughter better than anyone and felt certain that she could cope with the role. The Los Angeles Board of Education and Welfare, however, took a different view and their loudly voiced doubts almost lost Jodie the chance to play the part of Iris.

Brandy was not the sort to roll over and agree with them. This part was too important. She knew Jodie was well able to cope with it, but in order to convince everybody else that she wouldn't be mentally damaged for life Jodie was asked to submit to a psychological examination. That, of course, outraged many people, and one columnist wrote that it was Brandy who should have been submitting herself to investigation by a psychiatrist for allowing her daughter to be subjected to such an ordeal. Jodie took the whole episode with her customary composure.

'I spent four hours with a shrink to prove I was normal enough to play a hooker. It was the role that changed my life. For the first time I played something completely different. But I knew the character I had to play – I grew up just three blocks from Hollywood Boulevard and I saw prostitutes like Iris every day.'

If Brandy's single-mindedness in getting Jodie that role shocked people, it paid off. Jodie was pronounced 'stable' by the psychiatrist and her performance won her universal acclaim and an Oscar nomination for best supporting actress. However, it also attracted unwelcome attention from a disturbed young man called John Hinckley.

Yet Brandy's determination did not always work. When Jodie was still just fifteen her mother heard that Robert de Niro was searching for a sexy and beautiful actress to play the leading female role in *Raging Bull*, and started to hustle for it. She asked a photographer friend, Emilio Lari, to take some sexy shots of Jodie. Lari obliged, with some reservations. 'I thought, "Oh, my God – I'm in trouble." You see, Jodie was just a small, fat baby – not very attractive or sexy.' A reluctant Jodie posed by a swimming pool with a towel draped round her. 'She was dead set against doing it. She was only fifteen, after all. And she only came around after a lot of persuasion from her mother. I was allowed to take the pictures because I was a friend and because she trusted me.'

The results were stunning, but not what Robert de Niro was looking for. Jodie looked sexy all right, but it was the sexiness of a nymphet Lolita and not that of a grown woman. She didn't get the part. It was also the last time Jodie ever stripped for a camera until *Nell*. She's just not comfortable with nudity. Her sister Connie stood in for her in the nude scenes in *The Little Girl Who Lived Down the Lane*.

In interviews Brandy defended herself vigorously against accusations that she pushed Jodie too far and made her take on parts that she was emotionally incapable of coping with. 'I think you have to know your child and her moral capacity. I have an older daughter who is gorgeous and talented, but she could never do what Jodie is doing, nor would I let her. There's an old Italian saying, "You will die the way you were born", and social studies bear this out – that the child's personality is formed in the first six months of development.'

Brandy totally rejected the notion of herself as the pushy stage mother. That old chestnut went out with the days of the big studios. 'Everybody mentions Judy Garland. Well, there were a lot of survivors too. Freddie Bartholomew is a successful businessman today. Many are happily married. Those kids who went off the deep end would probably have done so if they never went into films. As a parent you have to ask yourself, "Who is this for? For you or for her?"

'Besides, it's the only way I could bring up the kids in the manner in which I wanted to raise them. Good food, good schools, some financial security. And most importantly, the time to spend with them as a parent.'

Jodie, too, is dismissive. 'Judy Garland was one in a thousand. She was not a stable person and she had a crazy mother.' She believes she was probably the only one of the family to be the whole focus of her mother's attention. 'With the others Mother was always yelling, "You're not going to the movies!", but I guess when she got to me, the last baby, she decided she was going to be nice.

'I know I've grown up in the best environment. It is important to have art, knowledge and education put to you while you are growing up, even if you don't understand things. Maybe with her other children my mother didn't have time for that as much as she did with me.

'I feel very close to my mother. We're not like sisters because she still has the strong arm. She's head of the family, no mistake. But she's my friend, the one who guides me. She can be strict sometimes and if we disagree, which we don't very often – we have arguments, just like everyone else – in the end she wins.'

Inevitably there was conflict between Brandy and the young star as she progressed through adolescence to adulthood. Such an intense closeness at one point became stifling. Jodie's late teenage years were particularly painful as she coped with the aftermath of John Hinckley's attempt to kill President Reagan in a bid to impress her. There were rows and bitterness as Jodie tried to break free from Brandy's dominant influence and become her own woman, but Jodie tends to brush off the memory as just part of growing up. She told one interviewer: 'Sure, there was a time when I hated my mother. It lasted for about six months. I think I was thirteen. We were in London. I was making a film called *Candleshoe*, but she was having a really good time and I wasn't. She had friends, she was looking really good and she was happy. My body wasn't nice, I hated the clothes I wore and my nose was too big.'

It was a temporary estrangement but, although they are closer than many mothers and daughters, that early intensity was never to return, and certainly what the adult Jodie perceived as a brief passing phase was spread over several years. 'I regret that period where I just really hated having my mother around. We're so close, the best of friends. I scream at her and she'll call me four-letter words. I'll cry and she'll cry and I'll tell her to shut up. She still comes with me on sets and helps me make decisions. I do love her but I don't want to live with her for the rest of my life,' said Jodie.

Inevitably Jodie's career put a distance between her and her siblings. It wasn't that she didn't love and care about them. It's just that their lives were very different. Once, when Jodie was about twenty-one, Brandy suggested setting up home together like the Jackson family. Jodie put her foot down firmly. A family holiday in Spain was enough to convince her that it was a bad idea.

'Forget it. I mean, I love my brother and sisters, but we are so different – all of us. This is a horrible thing to say, but when I went to Spain to see them all, and I walked into the little house they had rented and it was all clean – c'mon, there were like six people living there! All the beds were made, there was Windex on the windows, my mom had on her whatever – it was like Dad coming in. It's the strangest feeling. I guess they haven't seen me very much so they don't know how to deal with me.'

Jodie has bought her mother a lovely home in Hollywood and frequently pays tribute to her in interviews. But while she still discusses her plans with Brandy, Jodie now makes her decisions on her own.

'The truth is that people who aren't raised in single-parent families don't know what it is. Your brothers and sisters are all fighting for the attention of one person and there isn't the unity that a mother and father would have to shield each other from it. It's a very, very intimate relationship – in some ways, overly intimate.

'My mom and I would sit and talk about everything. That was our bond. That was our tie. It was all about staying within four walls and discussing things. So I haven't lived a normal life but I think I've lived a very healthy one.

'We don't see each other as much and I keep stupid things from her, just so that I have something of my own. Like I won't tell her the gardener didn't come. The greatest thing my mom ever did for me was to empower me with this delusionary confidence.'

Looking back at Jodie's childhood now with the benefit of hindsight, it is easy to agree with Brandy that Jodie missed very little of the growing up that other children had. Brandy simply set about it in her practical way of making the best she could of her situation as a single mother. Living in the film capital of the world with two of her four children able to earn a living, the path she chose was the obvious one.

Said Brandy: 'It's a very lucrative business. Don't forget I have had four children to bring up, to support and educate. The two careers – Buddy's and Jodie's – have enabled me to spend more time with all the children because I haven't had to work in a department store and come home exhausted. I have been able to maintain the same standard of living we had when the marriage broke up. All of my children were educated in fine schools.'

Jodie still has her own room in the house she bought for her mother in Hollywood. She retreats there once or twice a week even now. 'I need to be with someone who loves me and who I can come home to every night and that might as well be Mom. My mother's the one person who doesn't give in to my propaganda.

'Look, my brother supported the family for a while and then I did and unconsciously I felt the weight. And, yes, I do look at her house and think, "I bought that." But Jesus, she's been through so much and has sacrificed so much for us, it's great to be able to give her what she loves and deserves. The great thing about my mother is that only one thing is important to her, that I'm healthy and happy. Everything else is weighed against that.'

The combination of factors that contribute to the mature Jodie's character are as diverse as they are interesting. From the moment she was born she has had the unsparing devotion of her mother, and Brandy's influence on her earlier career was overwhelming. During Jodie's formative years, Brandy quite simply gave up her own life to run her daughter's and, although many think of her as a pushy stage mother, Jodie is totally loyal to her and aware of the debt she owes her. In fact she glories in the slightly eccentric and bohemian lifestyle her mother created for her.

'Sure, not having a station wagon and two parents pushed me to be certain things and kept me from being others. But I am not going to say, "Gee, I wish I had that", because then I wouldn't be who I am. I would be someone else, which is OK, but not who I am. And I like who I am.'

Brandy's influence on her talented daughter cannot be underestimated. During the crucial years of Jodie's early development it was almost suffocating in its closeness. Brandy was a dominating figure who moulded her daughter's personality and helped her form opinions in the image of her own. Jodie could not help but take on board Brandy's interest in French culture and Japanese cuisine, her thirst for knowledge of world events, even her independent and at times critical view of men.

Jodie's view of life was coloured by her mother's, and this made her wary of marriage and commitment at an early age. Growing up as she did among a coterie of divorced and vengeful women made her feel protective of her mother, and Jodie put on a good show of not needing a man about the house or a father figure. She came to believe that she could live a perfectly happy and fulfilled life without such a restricting relationship as marriage.

Her early influences certainly helped her to develop an analytical mind. She also learned how not to show her feelings, to protect herself from the outside world by keeping the chinks in her armour to a minimum. And it laid the foundations for a steely strength of character that she is still building on.

TWO

Lucius Foster – The Father She Never Had

If Jodie missed the company of her father she never gave any sort of indication that she did. Brandy, who knows her better than anyone, genuinely believes she did not. 'It mattered very much more to the other three because they had known him before he left home. But he abandoned us before she was born and so she never really knew him.'

When asked about him, Jodie tends to be brusque. At fifteen she had a pat and slightly defensive answer to questions about her relationship with her father or lack of it. 'My parents were divorced when I was nine weeks old. They separated when I was minus two months. Sure, I've met him a few times. He remarried once and divorced again. It's not as if he's really my father. I try never to mention him. I wouldn't recognize him in the street if I saw him.'

Her defensiveness was undoubtedly due to her intense loyalty to her mother. From the day Jodie was born she never heard her father praised or talked about affectionately by Brandy, whose pain and bitterness over her failed marriage were so deep-rooted that she would have been much happier if nobody had ever mentioned Lucius again. The bitter rows over his infidelities ceased with his departure from the family home, but they left a nasty taste.

Jodie could not have been unaware of those feelings, and whatever curiosity she felt about her father in her early years was quickly suppressed. 'No, I don't miss him. Why should I? It's cruddy having a man around the house. You can't walk around without clothes, and a man means more dishes to wash,' was another of her smart-alec replies to the curious.

Later she began to rationalize the situation, eventually viewing it as a positive influence in her life. 'I feel lucky in a way that I never knew a father, that there was never a marital conflict in the house. I've always felt like a replacement . . . that I took the place of a husband, room-mate or a pal.'

She hardly ever sees Lucius, although they have met more than the four or five times she usually admits to journalists – mainly at family occasions such as the weddings of her sisters and brother. But he plays no part in her life at all. As far as Brandy is concerned the family was well shot of him. He broke her heart and left her penniless. To her he was a worthless womanizer whose carelessness with other people's money matched his irresponsibility towards their emotions.

Buddy, who is closest to him, described him as 'a bit of a bum' but was loyally prepared to make excuses for his behaviour. 'He's more of a dreamer than a crook. He has always been a dreamer. He was a genius too. He tested at genius level. But with business he just couldn't put it together. He always had grandiose schemes. He's a great people person, very outgoing. Everybody loves him. He's a charmer. If he was a con man he would have fled the country. He was there for me when it mattered. He gave me a job when I needed help, and he phones me just to see how I am. He was on the phone immediately after the earthquake.'

Lucius Foster is balding, portly and seventy-one years old now, but there is still a striking resemblance between him and his daughter Jodie. It is still possible to see how a youthful Brandy fell in love with the dashing former RAF fighter pilot. He lives in a house he designed and built himself, in a leafy, winding drive in North Hollywood, with his third family – his Chinese American wife Madeline and their two attractive children, Lu'chen, thirteen, and her four-year-old brother Azia.

Lucius is philosophical about the way he has been depicted as a bit of a monster by his ex-wife over the years. He denies he was ever a womanizer. Said Buddy: 'There were always other women. He had three sons before us and two more children after us and he walked away from all but the last two. These days he enjoys doing the father thing and takes them to school. Jodie wasn't around when all the rows were happening. She never saw him. The only time I remember her seeing him was at my first wedding.'

Buddy was deeply hurt by what seemed to him to be his father's neglect, however, and remembers as a little boy waiting on the front steps of their house on a Saturday morning for his father to come and take him out. Time and time again his father never came. 'I waited and waited but he just wouldn't show. My mother would say, "He isn't coming, he just isn't coming."'

Speaking to Lucius now about the way he ignored his children makes him deeply uncomfortable. It's something he would rather not face, and these days he is the model father to his young family. He tends to stand one step back from responsibility. He talks of the agonies of Buddy's teenage years as if they had nothing to do with him and as if he was somehow prevented from playing an active part in his troubled son's life.

Lucius clearly feels regret that Buddy suffered so much, and hints that it was Brandy's unpleasantness which kept him away. Although he hesitates about attacking Brandy, he is resentful about the way his son was passed over in favour of Jodie. By the time Buddy dropped out, Lucius felt there was little he could do to influence him. All Lucius could do was wait and hope that his son would return to him of his own accord as he grew into maturity.

'I think the way she handled Buddy was improper. She attuned more to Jodie than she did to this poor little boy. Buddy went through a trial of fire to achieve adulthood. It was terrible, awful, but we had to wait for him to grow to maturity. Yet it led to better things. We are father and son now. We hug each other.'

Whatever impression he tries to give of his fatherly concern, he was a little vague when asked how many children he had with Brandy during their nine-year marriage.

'How many? I'm trying to remember,' he said absent-mindedly. After a moment or two he recalled, and talked affectionately about his brood. To give him the benefit of doubt, he sounded as if he meant it. 'I have always been available to them. I love all my children dearly. Whenever there has been a need, I am there for them.'

He talked about his two older daughters in a detached sort of way, once again as if their lives had little to do with him. 'Lucinda married a wealthy older man who comes from many countries and does many things. She is living the life of an American in Paris and is now divorced. She has two children and teaches English. Connie is the conformist. She is married to an attorney now and lives out at Long Beach. She too has one divorce behind her. She has two children and is very settled. Sometimes it takes a couple of attempts to get it right.'

Lucius talks with pride about Jodie, the daughter he scarcely knows. What he does know of her sometimes sounds as if it has been gleaned from newspaper and magazine articles rather than direct contact. He likes to think she inherited her brains from him and boasts that 'all my children are gifted'. 'Jodie is a lovely person. Her whole life is film. I have never seen her do a bad thing. Her film crews are always impressed by her because she knows their job.'

He acknowledges the part his former wife has played in the moulding of Jodie's career. Brandy, he says, was a typical 'movie mother'. 'Jodie's mother was a very big influence on her life. They are very close friends. Jodie has inborn natural talent and tremendous concentration. Her mother has dedicated her whole life to this one child. I look for her to become one of the leading people in the film world. She was born with that single-mindedness. Her mother's influence is now waning. I don't think Brandy had as much in her as Jodie has. Brandy shoved her as far as she could. But it was something the child wanted to do.'

It's hard to separate the realities in Lucius's life from the Walter Mitty dreams. Cultured, intelligent and charming he certainly is, but he has a way of glossing over life's unpleasantness and detaching himself from the messes of his own making.

Lucius Fisher Foster III was born in Colorado, but lived most of his life in California, where his father was a wealthy property dealer. His childhood dream was to be a pilot and at the age of seventeen he joined the RAF, along with thousands of other young Americans eager to become heroes even before their country had joined in the Second World War.

'I was one of those strange little boys. I dreamed of the great day when I would be a fighter pilot and I accomplished it. I desperately wanted to fly. I was here, there and everywhere and served part of the time in the Far East. A lot of Californians joined up. They were short of people. I served in several squadrons. We all moved around a bit as people were killed. I was a fighter pilot in Eagle Squadron based for a time at Biggin Hill. I also served with 222 Squadron, nicknamed the 'Trembling Twos' because we were always frightened to death.'

Lucius rose to the rank of squadron leader, and once America was in the war transferred to the US Air Force, where he remained until 1954. 'By that time I was in opposition to what the national policy was.'

During the heady days of wartime he met and married a pretty British air controller – Margaret Ann McLennon. She was attached to 11 Group during the Battle of Britain. They were married for nine years and had three sons, Michael, Randy and Robbie, now grown-up and living comfortable middle-class lives in the Mid-West. Said Lucius: 'The eldest boy has met Jodie once, but Brandy got nervous about it and tried to stop it.' Brandy simply wanted to cut Lucius out of her own and her youngest daughter's life.

When he came out of the Air Force Lucius took the first job he could find, as a janitor, but quickly opted for a career as a real estate broker before settling into the construction industry. 'Finally I decided to do what I really enjoyed, and that was building houses.'

After his divorce from Margaret Lucius met Brandy at a fencing club. He prides himself that he was once quite an athlete, a skilled fencer. 'She came into the club one day and the fencing master introduced us.'

On paper the marriage lasted nine years, and the four children are evidence that there was a physical relationship right up until the end. But it was a stormy marriage, punctuated by rows and screaming matches over money and the other women in Lucius's life.

Lucius naturally views it differently, defending himself against Brandy's bitter accusations of his philandering. 'I was never a ladies' man. I'm fat, bald and over the hill, so I'm certainly not now. When I went into bars in London as a young flyer all my friends had a lady except me.'

His second marriage failed for other reasons, mainly because the couple were basically incompatible. Lucius claims he would have settled happily for a quiet suburban life, but Brandy's social pretensions and aspirations made his life unbearable. She wanted to move up in the world to mingle with the rich folk on the hill. Later she channelled these ambitions into her daughter's career. One way or another, Brandy was going to make it to a position in society.

So why do his ex-wife and son both say there were other women?

'They say that to protect themselves. Brandy wanted something else. She was going through hell. She was suffering so much. This little housewife wanted something that I couldn't give her. There was a lot of bitterness. I wanted a nice home with children and a lower middle-class wife. I couldn't get it from her.'

In fact Lucius is convinced that Brandy simply did not like men in general and him in particular. 'I don't think she has ever married again. I don't think she will. She was anti-men before she divorced me.'

He insists that he tried to keep contact with his children, but that Brandy was so bitter towards him that it became impossible. Once again he took the easy way out and stayed away. 'After the split with Brandy I had little contact with the children. It was not possible at that time. Brandy didn't want it. People go a little crazy at these times. They try to separate as much as possible from each other. It's hard to be objective. Brandy is a very emotional lady. Underneath she is quite a kind person. She just fights it all the time.'

He reminisced about taking Jodie on an outing, although she

has never referred to it in interviews. On one occasion, he claims, father and daughter talked frankly about his relationship with Brandy; but although Jodie is credited with enormous intelligence at an early age, it seems incredible that she should have been so articulate and perceptive about her parents' situation when she was three years old.

Said Lucius: 'There were the usual kind of outings where the father takes the children for pony rides. Jodie looked at me and said, "Listen, I never take sides." She was three years old when she said that to me.' His memories of typical family outings are at odds with those of both his ex-wife and Jodie. One or two such trips may well have grown in his mind as a whole series of them.

If Lucius indulges in flights of fancy about his emotional life, his business life has been at best disorganized and at worst shady. Several acquaintances and business associates have had reason to regret being beguiled by someone whom they regarded as a smooth-talking con man. Two British women, journalist Jillian Evans and publicist Edna Troman, were badly burned by the experience and took him to court in 1987, winning a judgement against him but with little hope of recovering their money.

Mrs Evans, who lives in Los Angeles, said: 'Lucius came up with a proposal to build apartments that would be affordable for middle- to low-income families to buy. A number of people who thought of him as a friend invested, with promises that we would make enormous profits within a couple of years. I put in $35,000 and Edna handed over $20,000. I don't know what the others invested, but they all gave over money because they thought they could trust him. He is a charming man who boasts about being in the RAF and also the CIA. He says he was sent to Japan and went through rigorous martial arts training there.

'The first thing he did with his new-found wealth was to build himself a house in Verbena Drive, where he still lives. He claimed it was for someone else, which would give him more money for the apartment building which was to be in La Mirada, a seedier part of Los Angeles. But he moved into it himself with his young wife, Madeline Leon.

'When we got the judgement against him he claimed he had never married her, but we all remember him going off to San Francisco for the wedding. Presumably he had put all his assets in her name. He claimed that she was just a woman he rented a room from.

'We used private detectives to uncover the tangle, and as they got closer to learning the truth Lucius changed his properties into different names, though money was never shown to have changed hands.'

The La Mirada building was finally completed but although some of it was eventually repaid investors didn't even get their money back, far less make a profit.

Said Mrs Evans: 'He gave Edna and me a strange story about his partner, a woman called Edele Singer, who he claimed had sold the building to Arabs for emeralds which proved to be worthless. We had gone through ten years of excuses which were a bit far-fetched, but this was going so far beyond credibility that we decided to sue.

'We got the judgement against him in 1988 and we weren't the first. There was one for $900 from a wood company in 1983 and another from a B. Cortesi for $300 in 1985.'

Transcripts of the hearing provide a revealing insight into Lucius's nature. While his memory is clear on some details, he is vague and deceptive about others. He couldn't remember how much his friends had invested and did not appear to have kept proper records, claiming that any he had were lost when his business moved offices. On the evidence he gave to the court he was either an exceedingly disorganized person or an out-and-out liar and con man.

His excuse for not paying Jillian Evans and Edna Troman their money back was 'pathetic' in their eyes. In a letter to their lawyer, he bemoaned the fact that he couldn't get on with earning his living because of the expensive lawsuits.

'How can I pay them if I cannot conduct business? I have suggested several ways for them to go, chief among which is to allow me to work so that I can make money and pay them. The present lawsuit effectively removes me from the arena in which money is made.'

In other words, drop the lawsuit and sit around waiting for their money back. The women decided they had been conned. It was everybody's fault but his and, although Lucius promised to pay back the money, the two women are still waiting.

Lucius and Madeline have been together twenty years now. They live quietly with their two children and Madeline helps her husband with his work as a building contractor. Lucius's health is poor and he takes pills for a heart condition. Occasionally, as is inevitable in the film capital of the world, they learn about Jodie's life from the hundreds of film magazines on the news-stands and showbusiness items on television.

It appears that the years have mellowed Brandy Foster's attitude to her ex-husband somewhat and there is now a kind of truce, though it could hardly be described as affection. Once, Jodie was driving through Hollywood with her mother when Brandy spotted Lucius walking down the street. Jodie remembers: 'She yelled out of the window, "Hey, Lucius, how about buying us a hamburger?" He did, and it was kinda nice,' she said.

Sometimes the third family Foster go to see Jodie's films. Once, by an extraordinary coincidence, they met up at the première of *Little Man Tate*, the film which Jodie directed. Lucius's daughter Lu'chen, whom he describes as 'a gifted child', won a competition to design a milk container at school. Her prize was a family outing to the première of *Little Man Tate*.

'We all met up at the film. Jodie stopped and talked to us there,' he said proudly, as if his famous daughter had invited them.

It seemed a little sad.

THREE

From Disney Moppet to Yale Freshman

If one thing characterized the young Jodie, it was the impression that she was older than her years. There was something in the candid blue gaze that seemed knowing and wise. It was partly her intelligence; a little to do with her experience growing up, as she did, among adults on the sets of one film after another; and a lot to do with her mother's influence. More important, it was just the way she was – naturally curious, critical and analytical, she was never prepared to accept either people or situations at face value.

But she was an unsophisticated child for all her exposure to one of the world's most hard-bitten cities. A more down-to-earth all-American kid clearly enjoying herself would have been hard to find. Even in her mid-teens her skateboard and a $1.50 yo-yo were her passions, and the only time she wore make-up was when she was working on a film.

Actor Scott Jacoby worked with her on *The Little Girl Who Lives Down the Lane* when he was nineteen and she was twelve, and was impressed even then with the way she handled herself. 'Jodie's incredible,' he said. 'She's not like a little girl at all. There's no child-actor front or any baloney going on. She's straight with you, just goes in there and gets her job done.' Prophetically he added: 'In the next five years she could be one of the big stars.'

Small and slightly built, with dark blonde hair and a gap-toothed grin, she already had a maturity and poise which had come from familiarity with her working environment. After all, she had been performing in front of a camera since the age of three. Her conversation was punctuated with giggles, but few people laughed when the youngster announced that she had four ambitions. 'I want to be President of the United States, I want to go on the stage, I want to go to Rome and I want to get a hamster.' Even at that stage in her development the White House was well within her reach, and few would have been surprised if that was the direction she took.

In the meantime she had a crush on Robert Redford and spent hours in her bedroom listening to pop music. She filled any spare time she had with physical activities – skiing, swimming, playing basketball and tennis. She joined a karate class for two years, hoping to get the better of her older brother Buddy.

'Once, my brother told me to get out of his room and I threatened to give him a chop,' she grinned. 'I used to be a bratty sister. The fights we used to get into! Like he used to burp real loud and say I did it.'

In the early years Jodie's relationship with Buddy was affectionately competitive, easy without being particularly close – two children who both happened to be television stars growing up together under the careful guidance of their mother who masterminded both careers.

Buddy was an appealing child, with his bright blond hair and cute, cheeky smile which made him perfect for *Mayberry RFD*, a family show about a little boy growing up in a rural area. But as he developed into adolescence, his voice broke and his skin acquired its regulation teenage pimples, he became less attractive to producers and work began to dry up. He found it hard to take, especially as the blossoming Jodie was never out of work and her value as an actress seemed to increase with each picture.

By the age of nineteen Buddy was working at the Beverly Hills Hotel parking cars while his baby sister was inside doing deals with producers. By this time Buddy had married a pretty Mexican girl, Diana, and moved out of the family home. He was also the father of a small baby and feeling restless and unsettled, although he still talked of himself as an actor 'between jobs'. Buddy's youthful marriage did not please his family. A close family friend said: 'They were not happy about it. Mexicans and Puerto Ricans are treated like second-class citizens by many Americans, and they felt Buddy was throwing his life away by marrying her.' The periods of time between jobs became longer and longer, until work fizzled out altogether. It took the young man years to come to terms with the fact that he was not a star any more.

Meanwhile Jodie was simply getting on with her life. It was hardly necessary for her to adapt to her split existence – in school and at work. It was all she had ever known. Her quick brain and exceptional memory made it easy for her to catch up on work she had missed when she was away filming, and whenever she was abroad she would have a tutor on set.

Occasionally the headmistress of the Lycée Français travelled with Jodie and her mother. The tall, immaculately groomed Madame Kabbaz was used to dealing with the offspring of famous film stars: the children of Marlon Brando, Telly Savalas, Petula Clark, Charles Bronson, George Segal and many others had passed through her classrooms. But no child had impressed her as much as Jodie from an academic point of view. She travelled with her to England for the making of *Candleshoe* with the late David Niven and Helen Hayes. It was exciting, even for someone used to meeting stars, to share a little of the lifestyle.

The Lycée provided a strict traditional education, with classes conducted in French. Jodie went there when she was eight, and within a few months was able to cope with the language. Once she had mastered it she sailed to the top of her class, where she stayed till the end of her school days.

Said Madame Kabbaz: 'We have taken her IQ. It is very high, but it is not our policy to reveal the exact figure. Certainly she is one of the brightest students we have ever had. She is intelligent, hardworking and the most well-balanced child I have ever known. To the rest of the world Jodie may be an object of curiosity and speculation but at school, fortunately, she is among many children of film stars. They help her to be normal.'

Jodie responded well to the school's firm discipline. She was punctual, with her uniform neatly pressed, a conscientious pupil whose work was always presented on time. She was, felt Madame

Kabbaz, well able to cope with the pressures of her dual life. Her tutor had plenty of opportunity to observe her and monitor her development. 'I think she is such an intelligent person and so enjoys what she is doing, both in school and with acting, that this, for her, is still a teenage time. I've also noticed that she is quite well able to insulate herself against the artificial value of the film business.

'When she's been on the set, and I've observed her, she has been interested in the direction, the camera, the lighting and the sound. She certainly doesn't subscribe to the idea of being a star – actually she just likes to make people laugh by clowning around. Also, you must remember that when she makes films for people like Disney it is still a child's world, although it is an adult business, because the actors and actresses are nearly all children. They may be acting in strongly imaginative plots with other children, but that is exactly how teenage children play with each other anyway.'

The combination of Madame Kabbaz's influence at school and her mother's at home ensured that the focus of Jodie's life was academic. The challenge that the French language provided was absorbing. There was no time for the young star to preen, even if it had been in her nature. At the Lycée she was never treated like a star.

Her friends would tease her about commericals she had appeared in – fifty in all by the time she was ten. She took it all with good humour: she enjoyed making people laugh.

Even when she began to receive sackfuls of fan letters, many of them suggestive and kinky, from men, it did not faze her. 'I just throw the weird stuff away. A woman answers most of the others. But when I'm bored I sometimes browse through them. They all seem to say the same thing: "You're probably not reading this because it doesn't get to you . . ." And in a sense they're right. None of them do get to me.'

Her face became increasingly well known. She was the little girl in the Crest toothpaste ad who ran up to her father on the golf course. She often appeared in pet food ads or as the cute kid munching America's favourite cookie – Oreos. In many she was the appealing child of a handsome all-American father, a situation of which she had, of course, no personal experience.

She became the mini-queen of television ads until Brandy decided enough was definitely enough and moved her on to proper acting jobs, much to the anguish of her agent who thought she was mad to turn her back on such a steady income.

In May 1969 Jodie made her debut in an episode of *Mayberry RFD*, the country-based TV sitcom which starred her brother Buddy. Her ability to memorize a script quickly and her professional attitude to work ensured that she was regularly employed for the next five years in a variety of sitcoms like *The Courtship of Eddie's Father*, about a father-and-son relationship, and *My Three Sons*, about a father and three boys, *Gunsmoke*, *Kung Fu* and *Julia*. Then there were parts of varying sizes in *Bonanza*, *The Partridge Family*, *Perry Mason*, Love *Story* and *Medical Center*.

During the autumn of 1973 Jodie made regular appearances as Elizabeth Henderson on ABC Television's *Bob and Carol and Ted and Alice*, and the following year she was in the television film *Smile, Jenny, You're Dead*. There were three hour-long programmes in a series for ABC called *Afterschool Specials*: the first was called *Alexander*, followed by *Rookie of the Year*, which won an Emmy Award – Jodie played the star role. Finally she did *The Life of T. K. Dearing*. Then she made a pilot for a possible series called *My Sister Hank*, playing the title role, for CBS, but it was never turned into a series.

In retrospect it was only a matter of time before Disney signed her up. Her first full-length feature film was *Napoleon and Samantha*, made when she was eight, co-starring a 550-pound lion which gave the slender child an experience which could have shaken her confidence enough for her to want never to work with animals again. Relating what happened years later, she went out of her way to defend the animal from what must have been an alarming encounter.

'I was going up a hill. We'd worked with the lion all day. He was very fidgety because he hadn't gotten a lot of sleep – kids had been shooting pellets at him at night. He was being pulled up a hill with piano wire and I got too close.

'His mane sort of reached around my body. He took me up by my hip, turned me sideways and started shaking me. I thought it was an earthquake. And then he was so nice. He put out his paw to protect me from falling and *pshwat* . . . it completely bruised my whole leg.

'He sort of turned me around. I was looking sideways and everybody was running. Everybody ran away.'

She doesn't remember the lion's teeth piercing the skin on her front and back, or how the animal's trainer managed to extricate her from its jaws. 'When I finally got undressed and showered there were two holes in my front and two in my back. So I got seventeen shots and had to eat broth and jello.'

Ten days later, after a short spell in a Portland hospital, she was back on set. 'And wouldn't you know, the first day I had to hold this rooster. He took one look, went *grrr*! I dropped the rooster and ran.'

She might have been a brave child but she certainly wasn't stupid. She could, of course, have quit the picture, but she reasoned that no real harm had been done. 'My mom left it up to me, but I think she felt it was smarter for me to go back – you know, to get back on the horse that bucked me,' she said.

It was just as well she did, as by this time she was the family breadwinner – her income from films outpaced Buddy's earnings from his television career. And she can't have been badly upset by the lion as she named her pet Yorkshire terrier Napoleon after him.

The part of Addie Pray in *Paper Moon* seemed tailor-made for the mischievous young Jodie, although Tatum O'Neal was the star of the successful Peter Bogdanovich film along with her father Ryan, who played the wandering Bible salesman. Paramount decided that Jodie was more what the writer had in mind than Tatum and cast her opposite actor Chris Connelly who played Ryan O'Neal's younger brother in the popular American soap *Peyton Place*.

It should have been a sure-fire success, but weak storylines and suicidal scheduling opposite the second half of the top-rated family show *The Waltons* caused it to flop.

Poignantly, however, Jodie struck up a warm relationship with Chris Connelly which echoed little Addie Pray's continuing search for her father in the series. He in turn adored the child, spending hours just playing with her, kicking a football, or going for long walks and talking with her. He even taught her how to drive a car although she was not yet old enough to hold a licence.

She gushed her childish enthusiasm for the young man, who resembled her hero Robert Redford. 'You can really talk to him and play ball with him and go on a picnic or learn to drive a car from him or have secret languages with him and sometimes you don't have to talk at all but understand each other just the same . . . The ideal father would have the looks of Robert Redford, the sense of humour of Richard Harris and the friendship of Chris Connelly.'

It was a time in her life when she might have missed having a father at home, but there were plenty of avuncular figures in her life who had real affection for the child. In any case, her intense loyalty to her mother would never let her admit to her loss, even to herself. She had plenty of friends, many of whose fathers had left the family home, to fill any emotional void. It was no big deal to her, not something she sat and wept over. She would probably have given it very little thought were it not for the fact that every journalist who interviewed her asked her about it.

For the moment Jodie was just being a kid, both on screen and off, but gradually her screen roles were beginning to change as Brandy steered her skilfully away from being merely a child star. Inevitably there were comparisons with the precocious Tatum O'Neal, and there was undoubtedly rivalry. Writer Patrick Pachecho spent several days with Jodie and her mother and remembers them talking about Tatum in a critical and less than generous way. 'They weren't very complimentary about her. They were picking holes in a performance of hers,' he said.

For public consumption Jodie was, however, diplomatic. 'Everyone thinks we must be rivals, cutting each other's throats. Well, we're not. I met her once at the Academy Awards and she was very

nice. There's no competition between us. We do completely different things. She's younger than me. You adults are always looking
for a drama that's not there.'

Jodie's television work continued alongside the film career for a
few years. On the whole the roles were undemanding: she just
played versions of herself. In Disney's *One Little Indian* she had a
small supporting role as the daughter of a handsome widow in a
tale of the Old West. In her first film for adult audiences – *Kansas
City Bomber* (1972) – the ten-year-old Jodie was the neglected
daughter of a roller derby queen played by Raquel Welch.

Then there was another juvenile film – a musical version of
Tom Sawyer. Jodie received mixed reviews for her role as Becky
Thatcher. *Newsday*'s Martin Levine wrote that 'her vocal intona-
tions and facial expressions, especially, are charming – but it's the
charm of someone two or three times her actual age of nine'.
Richard Schickel in *Time* was kinder. 'Only Jodie Foster, as Becky,
suggests that she somehow remembers what it is like to be a real
person in a real world.'

Child actors are inevitably compared with the biggest child
actress of all – Shirley Temple – and Jodie was no exception. She
was, however, a million miles away from Little Mary Sunshine.
She saw herself as an updated version of the sugar-sweet child
whom everybody loved.

'I still play a sweet little kid. It's just that my sweet little kid is
modernized. The Shirley Temple kid doesn't sell any more. But I
don't think I'm so different from her. I think that kids always have
been smarter than adults think they are. Maybe the difference with
me is that my characters show that a little more.'

It was *Alice Doesn't Live Here Any More* which first brought
her into contact with director Martin Scorsese and started her on
her path away from the wide-eyed roles of the Disney films. It
wasn't a big part – the real stars were Ellen Burstyn and Kris
Kristofferson – but Jodie's portrayal of a wine-swilling street urchin
impressed Scorsese so much that he thought of her immediately
when it came to casting the twelve-year-old prostitute Iris in *Taxi*

Driver. For her starring role in *Alice* Ellen Burstyn won an Oscar for best actress of 1974. Jodie was described by one reviewer as 'looking like a boy and talking like a man'.

After *Alice* there was a two-year period when Jodie did not make any films, but Brandy was always searching for the right role for her. When it came along, Brandy was uncertain at first. On first reading the script of *Taxi Driver* Jodie, then aged thirteen, was also unsure, and both she and Brandy wavered about whether she could handle it. Their reasons were rather different. Said Jodie: 'At first I didn't want to do the part, but only because I was worried my friends would tease me about it afterwards. I thought, "Wow, they've got to be kidding." It was a great part for a twenty-one-year-old, but I couldn't believe they were offering it to me. I was the Disney kid. I thought, "What would my friends say?" I could just hear their little snickerings, so I didn't want to do it. I never worried about doing it on moral grounds and nor did my mother. Her main concern was whether I could handle the role as an actress. I had never played such a serious part before.'

If she had known how closely she was to be put under the microscope as a result of taking on that role, Jodie might well have had second thoughts. She found the whole row over whether or not she was going to be emotionally scarred by the experience utterly ridiculous.

Barely into her teens, she was being asked by adult reporters and television interviewers to explain her views on everything from child prostitution to the effectiveness of the California educational system.

She would sigh deeply and say: 'Some of the questions are real dumb. I mean I'm just a kid. Who needs my opinion? A girl I played once had a line that goes "I get up every morning with my dukes up." That's how I'm beginning to feel. I act in the movies.. It's just a job. I don't make a federal case out of it, and I wish people would stop making a federal case out of me. They'll make me think I'm some kind of freak.'

Jodie regarded the concern for her moral welfare over the

exposure to prostitution with scorn. She put up with sessions with psychologists from the Los Angeles Welfare Board because she knew she had to in order to be allowed to do the movie. She complained later: 'I spent four hours with the shrink to prove I was normal enough to play a hooker. Does that make sense? He asked me what kind of food I ate and would I like to get married. I said not at thirteen.' The psychologist's reaction to this thirteen-going-on thirty-year-old's barely concealed exasperation is not recorded.

Jodie was probably no more or less sophisticated than any teenager and just as curious about sexuality, although not in the least interested in dating at such a young age. 'I don't know why adults are so shocked that kids know about sex. Most of us know what goes on from the age of ten. You can't help knowing when you live near Sunset Strip with all its massage parlours and male and female hookers hustling out in the open. Anyway, I think brothels should be made legal. If men want to go there, let them. Adults think that all kids have to do is whisper about sex. Well, we don't. It's the adults who are obsessed with it.'

She defended her mother fiercely against accusations of irresponsibility in letting her take the part. 'I think you've got to know your kid. My mother thought I was ready to handle it and I thought I was too. I'm sure a lot of kids wouldn't have been.'

When Brandy first saw her daughter in the satin hot pants and six-inch platform shoes she was as impressed as everyone else and just as disturbed. 'I couldn't believe how she looked in her wardrobe. Suddenly she had legs. I don't think I'd ever seen her with her hair curled. I was very happy when she returned to her grubby little self.'

Meanwhile the Hollywood gossip machine buzzed with rumours that the child had gone out on to the streets of New York to do some research observing first-hand how prostitutes operate. 'That is nonsense. I never did anything of the kind. They did bring a young hooker along one day to give me some hints on how to act, but I found her too much of a cliché. Otherwise I didn't do any research. I just played the part the best way I could,' she said.

'I'd like to say I studied and concentrated and researched and that it all just came out of me. But I'm no method actor. In fact I've never even had an acting lesson. If anything, what I do is by instinct. My method is just do what I think is right. I don't think you have to feel the character and research it for years. Maybe I would do research if I were playing Henry VIII, but otherwise no.'

The fact that Iris was a prostitute was almost incidental to Jodie. She was more interested in why Iris had ended up on the streets. 'I didn't see myself as a baby hooker, but as a runaway, a sad character,' she said.

Just in case the young actress might have been corrupted by the experience, the Los Angeles Welfare Board sent a social worker to the set every day to keep an eye on her. It was hardly necessary. Jodie was more interested in the shooting scenes than in the prostitution, and even then it was the technicalities that fascinated her rather than the violence.

'There was a welfare worker on the set every day and she saw the daily rushes of all my scenes and made sure I wasn't on the set when Robert de Niro said a dirty word. Actually I think the only thing that could have had a bad effect on me was the blood in the shooting scene. It was really neat, though. It was red sugary stuff. And they used Styrofoam for bones. And a pump to make the blood gush out of a man's arm after his hand was shot off.

'Anyway nothing really happened in my scenes, at least technically. I didn't say a single dirty word and nothing went on sexually. The welfare worker didn't care about all the violence in my scenes. All she cared about was the sex.'

The do-gooders, however, were just as worried about the child's exposure to the wicked world of Hollywood movie stars, drink, drugs, sex and the psychological problems which have led to overdoses or slashed wrists in overwrought young women.

Jodie laughed at the thought of herself doing anything like that. She gave film critic Gene Siskel her fifteen-year-old philosophy on life in a *Chicago Times* interview. As usual she talked in a non-stop flow of chatter, punctuated with giggles, sometimes sounding like a woman twice her age and suddenly lapsing into cheeky childhood: 'I hate the taste of liquor. I prefer chocolate cake. I don't like drugs 'cause everyone's doing 'em and it looks stupid. And sex? You know, if my mother was around she'd take a swing at you for asking these questions. I don't even have a boyfriend, but I wouldn't tell you if I did anyway.

'And what's the other one? Right, suicide. Well, I don't expect to die for a long time. When I do, it'll probably be in a car accident, because I drive really lousy.

'No, I'm not sixteen yet. I'm only fifteen and a half. So don't tell anyone I drive. They'll put me away. What do I drive? It depends what's around. I drive one of my friend's Mercedes. And that's really fun, 'cause it goes real fast. Sometimes I drive my mother's Peugeot. And when I'm in Paris I drive a mini-car.'

Iris was a turning-point for Jodie. Up until then she had found her craft easy. She would turn up, learn her lines and just be more or less herself. This film was different. It required a great deal more from her. Her physical appearance was just at the right stage of development to portray the street-wise runaway from Pittsburgh – long, skinny legs emerging from hot pants and perched on platform shoes, world-weary eyes ringed with dark circles, and a straw hat, brim upturned, pulled down over her curls. The image was strong – child-woman, scamp-vamp, a blend of innocence and precocious sexuality.

'That film completely changed my life. It was the first time anyone asked me to create a character that wasn't myself. It was the first time I realized that acting wasn't this hobby you just sort of did, but that there was actually some craft.'

She knew she had to be more than good in the role of Iris. As always in her life Jodie was aware of the consequences of everything she did and how the world would see her. 'I had to be really perfect or it would ruin my career. That role was really risqué for a child,' she said.

But it wasn't just a good career move. The film crystallized her attitude to her profession. 'Until four years ago I just thought of acting as something to do. I figured when I got older I'd be a lawyer and President of the US. I'd always hated all my movies. I'd never felt good about anything I'd done, and then I did *Taxi Driver*.'

Martin Scorsese admitted that when he first met her at the auditions for *Alice* he thought Jodie was a boy, but he fell for her deep, husky voice immediately. 'In came this little girl with a Lauren Bacall voice. She cracked us up,' he said.

He was prepared to put up with the lengthy deliberations of the Child Welfare Board to be able to use her on *Taxi Driver*.

'I never had any doubts. She's always very fresh and very clear in her personality. When we were shooting in some of the rougher areas of New York on location I was more worried about the effect it was going to have on some of my more adult performers than on her. She takes direction extremely well and has a natural craft, a natural capacity when acting, which is a delight. In one scene she plays with Robert de Niro, they're in a café together and she has to pour sugar on top of jam on her toast, and she does it in such a way that it is not only childish and natural but it is also sophisticated and sensual. She was the master of that scene.'

Jodie in turn admired both Scorsese, whom she calls Marty and who became a friend, and de Niro, whom she calls Bobby. 'You rarely have a director like Martin Scorsese or a co-star like Robert de Niro, who rehearses and rehearses until you get the feeling that for the time you're with him he *is* the character. It's so real it's frightening,' she said.

Respectful though she might have been, the mischievous kid in her was not above doing a brilliant take-off of the brooding star, which Scorsese filmed and sent to de Niro.

Scorsese himself was quite simply 'the most stimulating man I have ever worked with'. She was able to judge him both as a director and as a man. 'He chews his fingernails, scratches his head, pulls his shirt out, worries and worries and worries. But he does let you work out the part yourself. He's an actor too, you know. He worries so much about movie-making that at the end of every movie he winds up in the hospital with ulcers,' she added.

Her pride in the work she did on *Taxi Driver*, for which she was nominated for an Academy Award for best supporting actress, remains, despite the attempt on President Reagan's life which will be for ever linked with it. 'I think it's one of the finest films that's

ever been made in America, one of the most important films. It's a
statement about America. About violence. About loneliness. Anonymity. Some of the best works are those that have tried to even
imitate that kind of film, that kind of style. It's just classic. I felt
when I came home every day that I'd really accomplished something. We were working improvisation – half that film was
improvised.'

Her whole attitude to movie-making changed after that. Working with Scorsese and de Niro, she saw how seriously people she
admired could take their craft. De Niro especially made her think
the whole concept of the film through. 'I think the taxi driver
represents those people who are left anonymous in the crowds, the
loneliness. I guess there's a part of him in everybody, that part that
is waiting to go out and do something to be recognized, rather than
sitting home in a nothing apartment and poverty,' she said.

It was extraordinarily perceptive for a thirteen-year-old. Even
her mother was taken aback. 'Jodie, did you read that somewhere?'
Brandy asked.

'No, that's just what I think,' came the reply.

If the way Jodie handled herself impressed the professionals,
her reputation and popularity with the public was also growing fast.
Such admiration could not help but have an affect on the young
Jodie. While not exactly conceited, she was contemptuous of anyone
who was not as professional as she was, and in particular young
actors and actresses of her own age.

With fifty commercials, twenty or more television shows and
six feature films to her credit, there was no one of her age with
similar experience when she arrived in Britain to film Alan Parker's
spoof gangster film *Bugsy Malone*, a musical send-up of gang
warfare in 1920s' New York. Used to working with adults, Jodie
found herself one of two hundred children, many of whom had
never acted before. She was openly derisive on occasions, laughing
or letting out a huge mocking sigh when they forgot their lines or
stood in the wrong place.

The fact that she had her own dressing room and the two

hundred other kids had to share did not go down well, and they determined to cut Miss Airs and Graces down to size. The youngsters meted out a chilly and unsubtle but effective brand of revenge by turning the fire hoses on her, soaking her to the skin and bringing her down a quick peg or two. It was a lesson swiftly learned, and Jodie became more careful about playing the star.

She didn't forget the episode, however, and at the Cannes Film Festival the following year told film critic Alexander Walker about her experiences on set. 'Those British kids from north England are real bullies. They resented me, my jewellery, my fur coat, my car – even my dressing room. There were three dressing rooms, one for a hundred boys, another for a hundred girls, and mine.'

Jodie did manage to make one or two friends among the cast, but they were the young American actors. Scott Baio, the thirteen-year-old who played Bugsy, said: 'She's a good kid. When we met, we played ping-pong and we were immediately friends. We used to wrestle, too, flipping each other to the floor. She's tough!' Scott and another boy, John Cassisi, who played Fat Sam, made the mistake of calling Jodie 'a dumb blonde' and paid for their cheek in bruises. John got a karate chop on the neck and Scott found himself hurtling over a table.

So for a few months she was able to fool about at least with Scott and John. They would race around the location shrieking with laughter. Then one day Jodie, running full tilt, pushed a glass door that wouldn't open. The glass fell out. She said: 'I was scared of what my mother would say. But she just thought it was kind of dumb playing tag with a glass door.'

Despite all the fun and kids' games, in interviews Jodie would occasionally answer a question with what sounded like breathtaking arrogance. 'I don't want to sound conceited but, yes, I think I must have star quality. I'm not conscious of doing anything, but there are some people who give an extra something to the camera and I seem to be one of them,' said the thirteen-year-old. It may just have been her total honesty and ability to judge both herself and other people critically. She simply had not learned the art of modesty. Another truism which in later years she might not have uttered was: 'You shouldn't act unless you have a gigantic talent and you want to.'

At fifteen she was still more of a tomboy than a young lady, seldom wearing dresses, and preferring her jeans, tee-shirts and trainers. Clothes didn't concern her at all, although she pointed out to one journalist that her jeans cost $55 – and that was in 1978. Her favourite piece of clothing was a flat tweed cap which she wore most of the time, even occasionally in the bath. 'I only wear things that are comfortable and don't give a hang about fashion. And I don't go out with boys and have never been on a date. The truth is I don't like boys. Oh, sure, some day I'll probably get married but I'll never have kids. Never.'

The bit about not liking boys wasn't strictly true. Jodie often said things for effect. She did like boys, but not in a romantic way. She had become firm friends with Scott and John and visited the Cassisi family in New York, where she became addicted to Mrs Cassisi's spaghetti. She was just being 'cool' about boys.

She was, however, genuinely unconcerned about how she looked – so unbothered, in fact, that she turned up for an interview with Martin Scorsese in her school uniform, correctly reasoning that if the director was any good at all he would see whatever he needed to see in her without her trying to second-guess him by tarting herself up.

'I don't think of myself as a star. I certainly don't think of myself as a child star. I'm just an actress playing child parts. And then, when I'm older I'll be an actress playing other parts. I think I want, eventually, to be a writer – even a director. But I think I would like to do that and act too,' she said.

When she was nominated for her Oscar for *Taxi Driver* she had mixed feelings about winning. 'There are so many grown-up actresses working for so long who have never gotten an award. It doesn't seem right to give one to a kid. When I'm seventy years old they could give it to me and say, "This is for *Taxi Driver*".'

The nomination was quite an achievement for her, and she was well aware of what an Oscar meant in financial terms. 'I hate to sound like a business person, but if I did get an award, that would mean I could make more money because the awards are really a way to get your price higher.' Then the fourteen-year-old would surface with a comment better suited to a teenager, like 'An Oscar is great but it won't get me to the beach on a Sunday morning. I'd rather have a car of my own.'

She had a typical teenager's cynicism about roles for women. 'It seems to be women have to cry in every role – and if they cry well enough, they get an Oscar for it.' Years later she cried so hard that she burst blood vessels in her eyes, but she too got her Oscar.

There were no tears in *Bugsy Malone*, in which she played Tallulah, the speakeasy queen and girlfriend of gangster Fat Sam. It was the first time Jodie had played a really feminine role. Tallulah was a vamp with bright blonde hair, slinky clothes and dollops of make-up which Jodie loathed. 'I think make-up is yuuuk! It took forty-five minutes to put it on, and washing it off was so messy. I think it looks stupid on kids. They think they look sophisticated but it just makes them look dumb. And who wants to look older? I don't. I'm enjoying myself as a kid. I have a lot of time before I grow up. I'm in no hurry.'

She put up with the indignity because that's what she was paid to do, but showed merely a professional interest in how she looked on screen. She seemed totally without vanity. 'On screen I think I look a bit odd sometimes, but I don't brood about my looks that much. I suppose I'll get more interested later, but for now my idea of a good role is one where I can wear jeans and no make-up.'

Bugsy Malone director Alan Parker was amazed at her capacity to learn her lines. 'One morning she was in make-up and I went in with three very complicated pages of script which I had written only the night before.

'I went to tell Jodie that I had rewritten the scene and to take her time learning the script and let me know when she was ready. She took the script from me, read it through once and said, "I'm ready now." I didn't believe her and told her so. She said, "Try me," so I read the lines to her and she came back word perfect. Now that's total photographic recall. It's phenomenal and she has it all the time. What's more, she takes such an intelligent interest in the way the film is being made that if I had been run over by a bus I think she was probably the only person on the set able to take over as director. Her sense of timing, her knowledge about how to read a line, is the greatest.'

Parker admitted that he hardly had to direct her at all. 'My total direction of her consisted of telling her I wanted a cross between Lauren Bacall and Mae West, and she did all the rest.'

Although she has a pleasant singing voice and later released a ballad single in France, her only song in *Bugsy Malone* – 'My Name Is Tallulah' – was dubbed by a professional singer. It was considered safer to use someone with a trained voice.

Bugsy Malone and *Taxi Driver* were two of the biggest hits of the 1976 Cannes Film Festival and so was Jodie, partly because of her fluency in French which won over the super-critical French critics. And when both director Martin Scorsese and actor Harvey Keitel dropped out of their interview schedules, the fourteen-year-old Jodie took over with great aplomb and talked to twenty reporters one after another and often in French.

Her great value to film-makers was her versatility. It was impossible to pigeon-hole her. Her mother helped her to make careful choices, so that in that year she was a child hooker in *Taxi Driver*, Miss Tallulah in *Bugsy Malone* and finally a dying girl, Deirdre Striden, in *Echoes of a Summer*. Her screen parents in that film, Richard Harris and Lois Nettleton, attempt to reconcile themselves to losing their daughter.

Echoes was her eighth film, and *Variety* magazine's film critic observed that she 'brings a fanciful spirit and gutsy depth to the part. Her precocious, almost androgynous quality is well suited to the task of playing a child forced to be "old" at the age of twelve.' Then it was back to being the American tomboy in *Freaky Friday*, followed by *Candleshoe*.

Freaky Friday was the unlikely story of a young girl who temporarily exchanges identity with her mother (Barbara Harris), so that each could view life from the perspective of the other. It was a popular film in the Disney mould, and perhaps a surprising choice after *Taxi Driver*. Just when it seemed as if she was distancing herself from the cute kid act, here she was playing another one.

Based on a novel by Mary Rodgers, daughter of composer Richard, it tells the story of a wacky day in the life of Annabel Andrews, played by Jodie, a typically headstrong and untidy American girl who resents her neat and well-organized mother's attempts to civilize her. One morning at precisely the same moment they both wish they could change places with the other, and all of a sudden it happens.

It was the sort of frivolous comedy that depends heavily on convincing performances by the actors. Jodie's cool gaze and world-weary maturity were perfect.

Said Jodie: 'I think it's important for my career that I make all different kinds of films. I'm proud that I made *Freaky Friday*. I shouldn't just make one kind of picture like so many child stars of the past did. And I thought the idea of *Freaky Friday* was terrific. A lot of my friends think it's my best picture. I really like working for Disney.' In interviews the emerging young woman is at times inbelievably mature, for example when she is discussing *Taxi Driver*. Yet she is still a child and her natural effervescence bubbles to the surface frequently.

It was an exciting year for the fifteen-year-old. Apart from her triumph at Cannes she was asked to present the American television show *Saturday Night Live* and was interviewed by Andy Warhol.

Warhol was impressed. Typically, it was a ramshackle, crazy sort of interview, more like a conversation between two youngsters. Jodie turned up for lunch at the Hotel Pierre on New York's Fifth Avenue wearing blue jeans tucked into black leather boots, and a newsboy cap. She was unfazed at being interviewed by the famous painter and came across as a fresh and natural young woman. She even admitted being a little star struck at times – though not, it seems, by Warhol.

'It's funny. I've been in the business a long time, but no matter who I see I always get excited. I was sitting next to Henry Winkler and I went crazy,' she told him.

She loved *Starsky and Hutch*. Hutch was her favourite. She

didn't like the idea of marriage. 'It's got to be boring having to share a bathroom with someone.' Shopping was 'the most boring thing in the world'.

And did she think she was beautiful, Warhol asked her.

'My mother tells me I'm beautiful but I don't listen to her. I look at myself – I've got a gap in my teeth, I've got an ugly nose, I've got blonde eyebrows, which are the worst thing to have. I have eyes that go down like this, I've got a red dot in my eyes, I've got puffy cheeks, I've got straight hair.' She had clearly assessed herself with her usual professional eye, and it certainly didn't sound like false modesty.

Once again the subject of rivalry between herself and Tatum O'Neal was raised. Tatum had just started at the Lycée, where Jodie was late going back for the beginning of term. She had, however, been on to her friends to see how Ryan's daughter was getting on.

'The worst thing for Tatum – apparently, because I haven't been back to school – everyone came up to her and asked her for her autograph. And that can be kind of disturbing. When you first start school, you want to get away from that. It's very embarrassing. But nobody's ever asked me that. I was very unfamous when I came to the school, so they were all sick of me by the time . . .' She stopped before she could add '. . . I became famous'. That would have sounded conceited.

Fêted as she was by famous adults, personally she was far more interested in people who were not famous. On location Jodie would invariably strike up friendships with the technicians. She was fascinated by the technical aspects of movie-making and was constantly questioning the cameramen, the lighting technicians and the sound recordists. She actually found all that more interesting than the acting itself.

Her approach to her craft is disarmingly down-to-earth. 'Acting is just a job and I don't happen to think it's very difficult. I don't get nervous or anything. I just walk on cold in front of the camera – doesn't everybody? Of course I might get nervous if I were asked to act on a stage. I mumble a bit, and on a stage you have to play to so many people. But with a camera you play for just one person

– the lens. It's like acting for your own family – even if there are fifty technicians on the set. I just learn my lines and get on with it. I'm not emotionally drained at the end of the day because I don't go in for all that Method stuff, getting myself worked up and into the rhythm. It may work for other people, but not for me.'

If she couldn't muster up a few tears to order, she didn't worry about it. A sniff of ammonia or a touch of glycerine on the cheeks did the trick just as well. It might not have worked on a stage, but this was the world of films and Jodie knew that it all looked the same on the screen. 'Anyway, those old Hollywood kids never really had to act. All they did was look cute, love Mummy and Daddy and hug Lassie or their horse. Shirley Temple was never an actress.'

A practical attitude to the task of film-making made her very easy to work with from a producer's point of view, but she was not above making suggestions if she thought he was doing it wrong. Once, on the set of *The Little Girl Who Lives Down the Lane*, the fifteen-year-old came as close as she has ever done to throwing a tantrum, because she felt the producer wasn't doing his job right. It was another child-adult role in which Jodie played a teenager murderess, Rynn, an orphan who has an affair with another teenager and fends off the advances of a child molester. In one scene she spikes Martin Sheen's tea with arsenic, but she was unhappy and ill at ease when asked to be more sexy.

'I walked off the set. It wasn't temperament. It was the straw that broke the camel's back. In the first place this crazy producer kept saying he wanted me to pull my dress lower. I decided he was nuts. I used to tell him to shut up. Finally, one day he said, "We have to have sex and violence or the picture won't sell." So I said, "Well, I'm not going to get into that."

'A couple of weeks later I was told they were doing the scene and I wasn't in it. I talked to the producer and got emotional and started to cry because, well, I'm young, so I cry. And I walked off. I was really upset.'

Actor Scott Jacoby, who co-starred, remembered how upset she became during another scene in which the villain killed her pet hamster. 'Although they used a dead hamster for the scene she got upset anyway. She couldn't work for a couple of minutes until she got over it.'

It was a nonsensical plot, but Jodie impressed critics with her icy aplomb. The film is set in an unfriendly village where the young girl lives in a rented home with a father nobody has seen. Nobody seems able to pry out the self-assured teenager's secrets. Once again there was concern about exposing Jodie to the world of adult fantasies and about the effect they would have on her. Both Brandy and Jodie were adamant that she would not do nude scenes and her sister Connie, who was then twenty-one, was recruited as a stand-in for one scene which in the end was cut.

'There are certain things I won't do and one is to be filmed naked. I don't think the nudity was very valid in that movie. Maybe when I'm older and there's something worth showing,' she said with her usual refreshing frankness.

The reviews were extraordinary in their praise for the youngster, The *Daily Mail's* film critic wrote: 'I suppose there are some roles that might defeat thirteen-year-old Jodie Foster. Maybe Lady Macbeth or Cleopatra or just possibly Hedda Gabler – though I'm not too sure about that either. The girl is simply miraculous. No youngster has made quite such an impact since the 1930s when every major studio was being largely supported by the box office appeal of its child stars.

'The direction and script with hints of horror to come aren't quite up to its leading lady's flair for keeping two jumps ahead of the audience's imagination. Lord knows where she learned such a skill so young. It must come from pure instinct.'

All this praise washed over the young teenager, already a veteran interviewee. Unfailingly polite and courteous, she nevertheless frequently expressed exasperation at some of the questions she was asked by earnest journalists from around the world, who treated her as a curiosity worthy of minute analysis because of her child-adult roles. But even if she sighed inwardly she understood the value of publicity, considering the 'dumb' questions thoughtfully and giving articulate answers.

In her next film Jodie worked with Helen Hayes, who was once a child star herself and did not particularly like working with children. In *Candleshoe*, which also starred the late David Niven, Jodie played a street-wise Californian teenager who tried to pass herself off as the long-lost granddaughter of an English marchioness.

Accompanied by her mother and Madame Kabbaz, Jodie spent another summer in England, filming at Pinewood and on location at Compton Wynyates, a well-preserved Tudor mansion in Warwickshire which had been frequently visited by Henry VIII. When Jodie was not required on set, Brandy continued her relentless pursuit of culture, taking her daughter to Stratford to see Shakespeare's *Troilus and Cressida*, which Jodie pronounced 'not one of his better plays'.

On set she was, as usual, word perfect. After her experiences at the hands of her peers on *Bugsy Malone* it was quite a relief to be back working with adults, and she admitted: 'I don't feel comfortable working with children. Sure, they learn their lines quick but their timing is so different. With adults you give a better performance.'

The veteran Miss Hayes liked her in spite of her habitual reservations about child actors. 'I understand her ease and attitude because when I was a child actress it was all simply a part of my life, just as it is for Jodie.

'She's quite brilliant . . . hasn't put a foot wrong. Jodie is about the age I was when I became an actress and, of course, there are pressures when you're so young. She likes to pretend she has no nerves. But when we started the film, I thought I detected that she was a bit tightly strung. So I told her I was nervous and she confessed that she was too!

'I adored her, I really loved her. I haven't always loved the children I've worked with on the set, although I've never really detested them, like W. C. Fields – he used to kick them in the stomach and that sort of thing. But nevertheless, I don't think the usual child actress is very lovable.

'They are either good at their job, or not, but as personalities they are very unchildlike and difficult creatures to deal with. Jodie is quite the opposite. She is really very lovable in every respect.'

Miss Hayes, who thoroughly enjoyed her own childhood performing alongside some of the finest actors and actresses of the day, believed that the difference between a child star who made the transition to adult actor and one that didn't lay in having a sensible parent to guide their career.

'I had a good, wise mother who didn't push me, who didn't make me obnoxious to people. And I think Jodie's mother is realistic and wise in her selection about what is good for Jodie. Jodie's mother has a very healthy respect for Jodie's own intelligence.'

Niven described her simply as 'a little smasher'.

After their sojourn in England the Fosters decamped to France, where Jodie starred in a French–English co-production called *Moi, Fleur Bleure* which had the American title *Stop Calling Me Baby*. The filming was done in the Victorine studio in Nice, and the outside location shots in Paris. Jodie and her mother rented an apartment on the Île St Louis, and Jodie became a familiar sight riding her bicycle around the streets of Paris.

The distinguished American actor Charles Fawcett, now in his seventies and living in London, was in charge of the English version, helping the French actors with their pronunciation. He remembers how impressive the fifteen-year-old Jodie was from the start.

'When Jodie came on screen something magical happened. It was the same when she arrived in the make-up room or simply walked on to the set. She had just had a sensational success in *Taxi Driver* and it was apparent from the first moment that she really was the star of our film. In a modest and unpretentious way she gave suggestions to our director that he rejected at first and then cautiously used to quite good advantage.

'From my point of view she was a godsend. I had been hired by the producer Peter Reithof to write the English version and to see that the actors learned and played their role in a somewhat American way.

'Having been out of America for so long I hadn't the slightest idea how schoolchildren talked, and the story was mostly about schoolchildren. When I heard my dialogue acted on the set I was horrified. It sounded false and hollow. Certainly not very interesting. I beckoned to Jodie, and without a second's hesitation she told me, "She should say so-and-so and I'll say this and that", and when it was filmed on screen it was absolutely perfect.'

Foster had mixed feelings about France and the French. She lived there for nine months with her mother and still visits frequently to see her sister and her niece, to whom she is close. She enjoys speaking the langauge, but in her teens found the French themselves incredibly chauvinistic. 'I love the people but when you live there you realize how little humour they have. You go to a dinner where the boys talk about politics and the girls talk about clothes.'

The jaded sophistication of the Parisian jet-setters irritated her. 'Best cheeses, best wines, best movies, best this, best that . . . but they don't need to think of anything else. Suddenly you just lose yourself and then you realize that two years have passed. I had spent nine months there and I knew nothing of what was going on except in Paris.'

While she was in Europe she made *Il Casotto* (*The Beach*) in Rome for distribution in the States. After an evening at a pasta restaurant in Rome the young star was photographed walking along a street with her arm around the glamorous American actress Sydne Rome, who co-starred in *Moi, Fleur Bleue*. When asked if they would pose for a picture, the vivacious Sydne, clearly in high spirits, exclaimed: 'Since we're living in a climate of feminism, it's better to photograph two women together – the worst they can say is we're lesbians.'

It was the kind of off-the-cuff remark that was to send their publicists reaching for their smelling salts. Jodie, however, didn't give it a second thought.

It could scarcely be said that Jodie missed out on her childhood. She had her childhood – it was just fuller than most other children's. She was never a wild child or a young Lolita off the screen. Thanks to her mother's guidance she was able to grow up at the same rate both on and off screen.

'I've got something extra. I know how to talk to adults and make a decision. Acting has spared me from being a regular everyday kid slob,' was how she put it.

Alongside her skateboard and her formidable collection of books, her bedroom was filled with trophies and mementoes of her successes. By the age of fifteen she had already won a clutch of prestigious awards – the National Critics' Award, the Los Angeles Critics' Award, the New York Critics' Runner-up Award, two Italian Critics' Awards, a Golden Globe Award and an Academy nomination. Jodie was the darling of the critics, who seldom gave her a bad review. She was vain enough to read them all and honest enough to point out what they saw as her faults. 'I just skim through their reviews to make sure they write the correct things about me. I've never had a bad review, though one writer who interviewed me did mention that I had a big mouth.'

Maybe if Jodie had known what she knows now she might not have been quite so amenable. In an interview in *Vanity Fair* shortly after she made *Maverick* she reckons she was a bit of a martyr – she simply didn't know she could say 'No'. 'When I was a kid I just didn't think I was allowed to say "No". I didn't think I was allowed to complain. I would get really bad frostbite because someone had forgotten to give me socks or something and the pain would be excruciating, but I didn't want to tell them – I guess I thought I'd get fired or they'd be mad at me,' she said.

Whether she would have become a 'bratty' child star is debatable, and her acquiescence was always seen as professionalism. So all in all the early years stood her in good stead as far as contacts and reputation go. Jodie Foster could deliver. She never gave trouble, she learned her lines and she was punctual. That's what matters to producers.

When Desmond Wilcox was making his prestigious 1977 television documentary series *Americans*, in which he examined in depth subjects from all walks of life, from the country's First Lady to an immigrant, he chose Jodie as the film star even though she was still so young. For Wilcox she epitomized the American star. 'She was Judy Garland and Shirley Temple rolled up into one. I liked her very much. She is very intelligent, very bright and at fifteen she was the most aware interviewee I have ever interviewed. She was a young lady who was directed by Martin Scorsese, who is a very complex and demanding character – but she understood what he was doing. She has survived one of the most hard-boiled and lacquered societies in the world.'

The last two films Jodie made while she was still a schoolgirl at the Lycée Français were released in 1980 and marked a transition from cute kid to adult. In both *Foxes* and *Carny* she was allowed to play a teenager struggling with adolescence.

In *Foxes* she played the leader of a group of four tough high-school girls in Southern California whose troubles stemmed from their conflicts with selfish and neurotic parents. Jodie was the central character, sixteen-year-old Jeanie, who lived with her divorced mother (Sally Kellerman), and the film follows the mainly sexual adventures and experiments with marijuana of the four girls in their teenage years.

The film received mediocre reviews but also the now predictable rash of newspaper and magazine articles worrying about teenage morality and the use of child stars in such movies. Foster was defensive. It was as if everything she did needed to be special, to have a purpose, and she at least had to believe in it.

'People routinely say things like they've been living in their cars for three days. It's Disneyland on wheels. These kids are really victims, not bad guys. If people see this movie and say we're lousy kids smoking grass and freaking out, they'll be missing the point. The movie's about what an obstacle course it can be to reach twenty-one in one piece. I had a sheltered childhood. I know kids like this but I don't run with them. I went to a nice little private school.'

In *Carny* she was Donna, a lonely waitress who decides to give up her boring and unproductive job in a backwater town for what she sees as excitement in the form of a travelling show, the Great

American Carnival. The focus of the movie was the relationship between the two men whose devoted friendship is threatened by their love of the same woman – Donna.

The part was originally written for a woman in her twenties and Jodie, still only seventeen when she made it, seized upon the chance to prove to everyone that she could indeed make the transition from child to adult actress without going through a fallow period. There is usually a moment when producers realize that their young child stars have developed into young men and women and they don't quite know what to do with them. Jodie was determined to skip by that moment without drawing breath. She was dismissive on the subject. 'I passed that stage long ago. I don't think the roles in *Taxi Driver* or *Bugsy Malone* have been the so-called "typical teenagers". They all dealt with real feelings that a person of twenty-five, thirty-five or eighty might have.'

Around this time Jodie began to notice a subtle difference in the way people treated her. Things she had got away with as a precocious child star were now not so easily tolerated, and she realized she had to begin to develop some grown-up skills such as tact. It represented a crucial stage in her development – at this time many child actors fall by the wayside. Few are smart enough to take in the put-downs or detect the edge in adult voices, but Jodie was an exception. As her brother Buddy said: 'She was always way ahead of us in knowing what was going on and where her life was going.'

At seventeen Jodie reflected on the changes in her life and the attitudes of those around her. 'The thing is, when you're a child and you're working and they're paying you, you're treated as a prodigy. You say something or make some suggestion and everyone says, "How bright, how perceptive, how intuitive!" And then you grow up and say the same things and suddenly you're cocky or insolent – an "insolent young woman".

'When I was a kid I used to go to auditions in a tee-shirt. Like who ever changed their jeans for an audition? That's when you're a kid. Now I don't go to auditions. I go to interviews with producers. And I dress up a bit. And they say, "Stand over there, turn around, well, your hips are all right, yes, OK, maybe." And I'm standing there speechless thinking, "Hold it! *You're* on trial here, not me! I'm looking *you* over, mister!" '

Once again Jodie's brutal honesty and capability for self-analysis betrayed an inner arrogance and self-confidence that she knew she needed to control if she was to survive, at least until she was in a position to channel these characteristics where she wanted them to go. She was, however, struggling as far as Hollywood was concerned. Her career seemed to have sailed up a cul-de-sac and she was coming to the end of her high-school education. She graduated from the Lycée with honours, giving her valedictory speech in French.

Then, at the age of eighteen, she made what to strangers seemed like a very odd decision, but to her friends was utterly in character. She decided to drop out of Hollywood and go to university. It was something she wanted to do for herself, to expand her mind and get away from the frenetic madness of film-making. Financially she was secure enough to make the break, and she intended to continue making films during vacations. The ivy-clad walls of Yale beckoned, and she plunged gratefully into the richness of an academic life.

FOUR

Buddy Foster – The Casualty of Jodie's Fame

I f there has been a price to pay for Jodie Foster's fame, her brother Buddy has paid it in full. Buddy's story is a classic Tinseltown tragedy – the child star, famous and fêted, who suddenly grew into an awkward teenager and was thrown on the scrap heap before he had time to realize what was happening. One minute the blue-eyed blond-haired kid was everybody's favourite all-American boy and, if not quite the Macaulay Culkin of his time, certainly a household name. The next minute the phones stopped ringing and the agents were saying, 'We'll call you' instead of 'When are you free?'

But for Buddy, the rejection by the public was not his only problem. As his work tailed off, Jodie's career blossomed with her first Disney film, *Napoleon and Samantha*, and it seemed to Buddy that his mother was never there for him.

There seemed to be a constant round of interviews, lengthy trips abroad, exciting premières and film festivals which Brandy had to attend with Jodie. Buddy stayed at home in the care of his elder sisters and his career dwindled. He was devastated. His way of coping was simply to drop out, run away to the beach, become a surf bum and be with other kids in a similar position.

Buddy ran away from home at the age of fifteen, and there followed a series of events which could so easily have ended in tragedy – a motocross accident which resulted in heavy dependency on painkillers, two broken marriages, an accidental near suicide and long years of therapy which have helped him come to terms with his intense bitterness.

Now thirty-six years old and happily married to his third wife, Stacey, Buddy believes his life has levelled out. He has finally found a woman who cares enough about him to make him feel whole again. His business is thriving and he's even thinking of having another go at acting. But the scars are deep and one of the factors of Buddy's teenage unhappiness lies in the feeling that somehow he missed out on his mother's affection.

In physical appearance Buddy – real name Lucius Fisher Foster IV – is very like his famous sister. Just five foot five to Jodie's five foot three, he has darker blond hair and lighter blue eyes, but the shapes of their faces are identical and side by side they are very obviously brother and sister. Buddy has fashionable designer stubble and wears a gold hoop earring in his left ear. His teeth are a perfect gleaming white, capped when he was in his teens and a well-known face on television.

His schoolfriends nicknamed him Buddy when they were unable to get their tongues around Lucius. 'I told them they could just call me their buddy, and it sort of stuck.'

While Jodie's early life was fairly secure, Buddy's was filled with domestic disruption and strife. His father's uncertain business career meant that the young family was constantly on the move from one home to another. 'Compared to my life Jodie had a very settled upbringing. She lived in one house where we lived all over the place. We didn't have any money,' said Buddy.

Lucius's casual approach to his business affairs was mirrored in his personal relationships and his alleged womanizing caused bitter rows with Brandy. As the marriage deteriorated so the rows increased, and finally in 1962 Brandy kicked her errant husband out. She was left with a less-than-favourable attitude towards men in general and Lucius in particular and, whether it was deliberate or not, Buddy was to feel the backlash.

'It was a majorly abusive relationship, although not in the physical sense. My father had a lot of girlfriends during the time he was married, and I guess my mom just felt this major rejection by men. I felt it all coming down on me. When I got older I felt that I was the one who carried the whole family.'

He was just five years old when his father and mother split and the new baby, Jodie, was born. Yet his memories of the bitter years are strong and of course reinforced in conversations with his two older sisters. With Brandy fussing over her and Lucius no longer in the family home, Buddy felt the first twinges of the rejection that later nearly overwhelmed him.

Brandy, engrossed in her own bitterness and the need to feed the family, had little time to worry about her son's feelings of insecurity. She was brisk and at times impatient when he voiced his desire to see his father.

'Pretend he's dead,' she once snapped at the little boy. 'It's easier.'

Buddy paused and reflected as he realized how callous that sounded, then quickly said: 'It wasn't malicious. I just think she ran out of patience.'

'They were very bitter with each other. But I never remember my father saying anything bad about her.'

One memory is seared on his brain, but until recently it was buried so deep that only long sessions on his analyst's couch brought it to the surface. It was a scene of domestic anger and violence that made a deep impression on the young boy, but for years he could not bring himself to talk to anyone about what happened one afternoon when his father came home to pick up his things from the house. Unbeknown to his parents, the little boy was listening to very word.

'My mother and father were getting a divorce, and one day he came to get his stuff and I was hiding under the coffee table with a tablecloth down over the sides. My father and my mother started fighting and I could hear plates being thrown. She told him to get out.

'Suddenly this woman, a family friend, came out of her bedroom with a gun and stuck it to my father's head, telling him that she was going to blow his fucking brains out. This all came out in therapy and I have told my mother about it. She says I wasn't at home at the time, but I was. It's not something that you could make up. I had always remembered it but never talked about it.'

It was a friend who offered the family a temporary home when Brandy could no longer afford the rent on hers. Without any constant means of support Brandy sensibly decided to put her children to work in the only way she could. Her work as a publicist had already given her the contacts she needed and the eager world of advertising was always on the look-out for handsome children to feature in its campaigns.

Lucinda and Connie both appeared in ads but with Buddy Brandy struck gold. He was an attractive and appealing child with just the right brand of cute cheekiness to suit the ad-men's idea of the typical all-American kid. He was very much in demand and soon became the family breadwinner. One particular ad for green stamps featured the cute little Buddy holding two dumbbells and was plastered on billboards all over America. 'I got 90 per cent of the work I went up for. I would walk into the room and immediately relate to the product. If it was a toy my eyes would light up and I was excited about it. My first ad was for Kellogg's Cornflakes and I told them I really loved the cereal.'

To him it wasn't like work at all. It was just a bit of fun, and he delighted in being the centre of his mother's attention. Then came the break for Jodie with the Coppertone ad, and soon there were two little breadwinners in the family.

Buddy did thirty or so ads before Brandy decided to move him on to the more lucrative world of television sitcoms. It was a risk to make the child unavailable, but she felt it was worth taking because of the increased income.

Buddy's memories are slightly different. As the only 'man' in the family he was acutely aware of the financial struggle, and even at that age felt a kind of responsibility to his mother and sisters. With no father around he thought it was up to him to protect them, and he determined that he was going to go out there and become a famous actor. He couldn't bear the agonizing sound of his mother's tears. 'I remember her crying on the floor when I was a kid, just worried about how she was going to pay the rent,' he said.

'I told myself I was going to be an actor. I was the first to think of it and pursue it basically on my own. My next-door neighbour, a boy called Greg Shanks, was already doing it and I pestered everybody until they let me go along. I did really well. It was really myself who took the intiative. My sister Lucinda and I would go around together and she would tell everybody that I was an actor.'

Looking back now, Buddy is clear about his own motives. Hours of therapy have helped him work out that he didn't imagine his commitment to the family or how it all happened. His career took off and he plunged with vigour into the world of American TV sitcoms, catching up with his school work on set with the aid of a succession of tutors.

'I put up with a lot of disruption. There were all these tutors and I didn't go to normal schools and grow up with normal boys. It's something I was never given credit for. My mother used to tell me it wasn't for very long and I didn't earn that much anyway. To her it may have been just a few years, but to me it was something I was doing for my family. I liked the responsibility – I just wanted her to acknowledge it. That's all I was looking for. I wanted her to say she really appreciated it.

'I was considered one of the top child stars in Hollywood. One of the things I had going for me really well was that when I played kids of nine years old I was thirteen. Even when I was in my mid-twenties I could play seventeen- and fifteen-year-olds. I'm thirty-six years old now and people still say I look twenty-five.' Although Buddy's career tailed off in his mid-teens, he still got the occasional acting job into his twenties.

His list of television credits is impressive. He played Johnny Dow in *Hondo* for a year before winning, as a nine-year-old, the starring role of Mike Jones in the long-running series *Mayberry RFD*, which he played for four years. There were also guest parts in countless top series like *Six Million Dollar Man*, *Dragnet*, *Emergency*, *Alias Smith and Jones*, *Joe Forrester* and *Adam 12*.

'I wasn't a brat. I did the job and I didn't cause any trouble. I didn't allow people to wait on me hand and foot. I didn't think that kind of job was part of it. There are a lot of people who are extremely spoilt and treat people like shit. I didn't like that phoney part of acting and the actors who were cut-throat. I loved acting, but I thought it was important to be extremely professional and do a good job and not be a pain in the ass.'

It was a heady time for the youngster. He couldn't avoid being a little carried away with his fame when everyone around seemed to adore him. When he went anywhere people would stare and point at him, and he received hundreds of fan letters from childen of his own age.

'When it was happening to me I didn't feel normal. I had this need to go to state school. I was rebellious. I would go to see schools and have interviews and then put my feet up on the table and smoke cigarettes and they wouldn't take me in. I wanted to play with the kids on the block. Wherever I went, everybody knew who I was. I went to a parade in California and these girls were trying to pull my hair out. I was a little bit scared, but it was a big ego trip as well.'

Occasionally he would come up against the jealousy of his peers. 'I started noticing it in my early teens. Kids would want to beat you up. My mother would hold me and tell me they were just jealous, but I thought it was because they all just hated me. I wanted to be accepted . . . My mother is a very strong woman. She would try to explain things.'

Years later, when he started going out with girls, he was never sure of their motives – whether they went out with him because they remembered his early stardom, or because they knew that his young sister was Jodie Foster. 'So I always made sure they didn't know who I was. I wanted people to like me for who I really was,' he said.

The transition to gangly teenager was a difficult one for Buddy. His looks went and he was no longer the highly employable cute kid. 'There wasn't so much work all of a sudden. That was just about when Jodie's career started to take off. I would stay with friends when she and my mother were gone. Like any little boy I got resentful.

'I was the breadwinner and the one in the family who made all the money at a time when we had a father who paid little child support. I grew up with a mother who basically didn't like men. I think it was as a result of her experiences with my father. I felt an obligation that if I didn't support my family, then I wasn't the perfect child.'

With the onset of adolescence, Buddy began to strain at the leash. He suddenly began to be aware of what he was missing in the form of comradeship and ordinary childhood pursuits, and he wanted some of it. Without a father on hand and with a mother so tied up in his younger sister's career, rebellion was only a matter of time.

'When I hit fifteen I wanted to be a boy, figure out what it was to be a man with no father around. My mom didn't really know how to handle that, so all of a sudden I was left at home with my older sisters when she started going on more and more interviews out of town with Jodie. I felt kinda drop-kicked. Then I started rebelling and got into drugs and the whole thing that was going on at the time, and just little bit by little bit everything began to fall apart.'

With hindsight he can see how it all happened, but at the age of fifteen his pain was almost unbearable. He did the only thing he could think of to ease it: he ran away to the beach and teamed up with a couple of older boys who lived in an apartment in Santa Monica. There he was free. He could hang out, laze around the beach, surf and rid his mind of all the responsibilities of the adult world from which he had fled. The young men he lived with kept a brotherly eye on him, insisting he attended school and did his share of chores in the apartment, and to earn his keep he worked in a petrol station. Buddy also fulfilled his dearest wish to go to state school and be normal.

At the time he didn't give much thought to his reasons. It is only through years of therapy that he has worked out his feelings of resentment and anger towards his mother. He feels now that she abandoned him just like she abandoned his father, although it was actually Lucius who left the family home. The mature Buddy is now able to understand his mother's bitterness and says he doesn't blame her, but the pain still surfaces in his words.

'When I was sixteen or so I got this VW Bug and buzzed around the beach in it. I really kinda wanted out of it because I felt rejected, and my way of continuing was to just leave. I don't understand how that all happened. I think I really felt condemned by my mother, even though I wasn't. I just felt this whole man thing, that I was being abandoned, kinda like my dad, even though he wasn't abandoned. I felt punished. She is very bitter and had to figure out a way of making a living. And the living was off me first and my sister Jodie second.'

If Buddy felt betrayed by his mother's apparent rejection, it was nothing compared to the feelings of anger and frustration he experienced when he reached eighteen. Expecting to have access to the money he had earned as a child, he found that it had all gone. Buddy was devastated. 'When I discovered that all my trust funds had gone and I really didn't have any money, I started getting a real bitter taste in my mouth, because my whole life I felt that I was replacing my father.'

Clearly Brandy had no choice but to use the money Buddy brought in to keep her young family in food and clothing. There was nothing sinister about it, no deliberate plan to deprive him of his earnings. Brandy could have gone out to work herself and left her children with child minders but this way she kept them with her.

As a young child, Buddy would have had no idea of the strains on his mother. It is to her credit that all of her children, even Buddy, remember their childhood with pleasure. She made up for their lack of money with her sense of style and appetite for culture.

Any money coming into the house was quite simply family funds to be used for everyone's benefit. When he reached his rebellious teens, however, Buddy, like most other teenaged boys, was only interested in his own life. All those years he had probably given little thought to where the money which put food on their table came from.

He had assumed that the money earned from his television work would be there for him alone to spend and it was a severe shock when he learned it was not. It was like a physical pain which made him totally unable to relate to his family. He couldn't even bear to see them or contact them, even when Jodie was going through her own particular brand of hell over the John Hinckley episode.

'At that point I was really rebellious and I didn't see my family at all. It was like once a year at Christmas or Thanksgiving, and it would end up in a fight and I'd run out. So it's taken me a while to grow up, but it's something that you always miss. It's like being a doctor and you go to Medical School. You become a doctor and you spend all these years at it, and then all of a sudden your hands start shaking and you can't do surgery any more.

'It was the same kind of thing for me and it was real devastating, especially because I didn't have the support of my mom. I think that was really crucial.' Brandy, at that time, was simply trying to do her best for her youngest daughter, but Buddy was too hurt to see it like that.

If his life was difficult on an emotional level, Buddy had yet another battle to fight on a physical one – against addiction. During his late teens, hanging out around the beach, Buddy took up moto-cross, an exciting and dangerous sport which gave him the thrills he seemed to need, the 'close-to-the-edge' feeling that many young men experience.

This too almost cost him his life after a horrific crash in which he sustained multiple injuries, fracturing his hip, pelvis, two vertebrae in his back, all the ribs on his left side and his collar bone. He also suffered severe concussion and his left knee had to be reset.

The accident had a longer-term effect on Buddy, however, when he became addicted to the drugs prescribed to ease the severe pain he suffered. 'They put me on painkillers and I became extremely addicted overnight. I didn't even realize there was an addiction. It was like all of a sudden I felt at home. It killed all the emotional pain and the physical pain. So I really was hooked very quickly and it just tore up my life for the next six years.

'There were several prescribed painkillers, like Percadan and Vicadan. It was the same sort of thing that Michael Jackson suffered. It made me feel OK. It was the first time in my life when every time I was on it I felt great. I had no worries, I didn't feel a lot of pressure, and that was the problem. It was a drug that for the first time made me feel good. It was very difficult for me to get off it.'

When he understood how dependent he had become on the painkillers he tried dropping them, but found life unbearable. He said: 'I tried all sorts of support groups like AA and tried just giving them up. But four days later I would feel like I was going crazy. My joints would hurt.'

It was only when Buddy went into analysis that he learned the reasons for his addiction. He needed to confront the pain of his teenage years instead of trying to blot it out. 'I definitely felt rejected, although you can't say that had anything to do with it. We all have choices . . . but somehow I felt major abandonment. Here we had this child actor who was very big and made a lot of money, but somehow I felt major abandonment,' he said.

He needed to get rid of his feelings of bitterness and at one point he thought of suing his sister for his own loss of earnings caused because his mother had devoted herself to Jodie's career and neglected his. Even then his motives were not really mercenary: he was more intent on getting his mother to admit publicly that he had contributed to the support of the family.

Said Buddy: 'I was going to sue. It wasn't really for the money. It was because I kept being downed when I would bring it up. It was a rebellious thing. I did consider it but didn't go through with it, because I thought it would be more damaging for my sister than it was worth.'

When he was seventeen Buddy fell in love with a pretty

Mexican girl called Diana. It was almost as if he was searching for love and attention, but his mother did not approve of the liaison. If anything, that drove the young man into marriage.

With maturity Buddy can see that their differences in background and outlook made the likelihood of the marriage being successful slight. Brandy had strong ideas about position in the community. In short, she was rather unhappy that her one and only son had formed a relationship with a Mexican.

'The whole rebellion with my mother was about her ideas about what sort of social thing she wanted us to come from. Diana was Mexican. It wasn't that she looked down on her, but my mom always had this caste system thing. She felt that if you came from a certain type of family then you needed to marry into the same kind of social-economic stratum. Eventually the marriage didn't work, because some of that was true,' said Buddy.

In the space of just a few years Buddy had married and become a father, even though he felt that he had never had a chance to do his own growing up. He got himself a job parking cars at the Beverly Hills Hotel where his brother-in-law, Chris Dunn, the head doorman, owned the parking concession. Buddy was popular with the clientele, especially the women, but it was never enough for the young man who had once been a television star. He needed the money, however, to feed his growing family.

As the years went by, the differences in background and culture between himself and Diana became more and more apparent. 'I found silly things irritating, like Diana always celebrated Christmas with the kids on the morning of Christmas Eve, and I always believe that when you wake up on Christmas morning you have your presents. You grow up with certain things that you think are standards. I started figuring it out in my mid-twenties that Diana and me were a lot different. It just didn't work out, although we have stayed friends. I don't know if my mother was right or if she had instilled something into me that made it doomed not to work.'

Despite his teenage rebellion Buddy carried on his father's family tradition by naming his firstborn Lucius V. Diana was pregnant with Brice, now ten, when they split. It was an ironically similar scenario to that of his own parents' marriage.

Buddy still hoped for a career as an actor, but offers of work totally dried up after his appearance at the age of twenty-four, alongside Jodie, in *Foxes*. Even that was in its own way a disappointment. 'I went for the part of the kid that rides a skateboard, the role that Scott Baio eventually did, and I guess there was a conflict because me and my sister look so much alike. It would have been difficult for us to do all those scenes together when we aren't supposed to be brother and sister, so I ended up doing a small part in it.'

His second marriage, to Robin Giffen, was made on the rebound. It was a disaster. There was one daughter, Courtney Jean, who is now nine. She is much loved but wasn't planned quite so soon, at least not by Buddy. 'Robin was pregnant right after the honeymoon. I didn't make these choices. It was just a case of "Guess what? You're going to be a dad." I really love my children, but I felt these were choices that I wasn't making.

'She became pregnant again but had a miscarriage and I was pretty relieved. I guess our relationship was pretty much shot down after that. It was obvious that she wanted to have children and I felt maybe one day but not yet. I'd already had a few, but I felt I hadn't even grown up yet. After that I had a vasectomy.'

Buddy always had the niggling feeling that his second wife was attracted to the glitz, and the reflected glory of Jodie Foster's glittering star. After their marriage broke up Buddy was at his lowest ebb, shattered and broke. 'When she left me I didn't have a dime. I had to start again from scratch. I guess my whole lifestyle changed. There were a lot of negatives. It was very difficult. I had kids at a very young age. After all, I was just eighteen when I was told I was going to have my first son.'

Drained emotionally and financially, for a brief moment he considered ending his own life. It was never a serious thought, but while he was toying with a handgun he kept for protection it went off accidentally and nearly cost him his life.

'Robin told me on the telephone she was leaving me. I got to the point where I felt so desperate I tried to commit suicide. I had this .38 gun in the house for protection. I was throwing it from hand to hand and I ended up shooting myself in the leg. The next thing I remember I was under the table downstairs in the dining room. I was bleeding very badly. My oldest son, who was living with me at that time, came home and found me and I was rushed to hospital. I felt so abandoned again. I was at a point where I didn't know what to do. My whole life was falling apart again.'

After his divorce from Robin, Buddy determined never to marry again. He had almost given up on love when he met his third wife, Stacey, now thirty-five, an associate producer in a film production company. They live in a pleasant three-bedroomed home in Woodland Hills, not far from Jodie's home.

'Stacey is the first woman I've ever been with who is extremely supportive through the ups and downs. I felt that the previous marriage was more about what she would gain from our relationship. Stacey stuck in there with me and helped me to get through the problems. I finally have a female in my life who is supportive of me. That has helped me grow up. I felt that I wouldn't get that from my mother.'

Buddy feels he now has his life back on track. He's through the dark years and is stronger for it. Ironically, it was his father who helped him get back on his feet again financially. 'I started working for him on and off when I was about nineteen. Since I never had a relationship with him, I sought him out.

'When I went to work for him he wasn't a dad to me, more of a boss. He has never downed my mother, but she always downed him. All my sisters have downed him, too. I care for him even though he's a kind of a bum. He at least calls me at Christmas and called me after the earthquake to see if I was all right. He constantly reaches out to me and for me that's important.

'He's married now to this American Chinese lady called Madeline and they have two lovely daughters whom he takes to school every day. I missed out on all that.'

Three years ago Buddy got his own licence as a real estate

broker and builder, and now has a thriving business as a general contractor and builder. 'I wanted to stand on my own and I have succeeded. My business is going well and we are comfortably off.'

The therapy sessions are coming to an end and Buddy finally feels in control of his life. So much so that he almost feels ready to have another tilt at the movie windmill. 'Therapy helped me a great deal. We have got to a place where I think I have finally grown up at thirty-six.'

There are, however, a few more ghosts to exorcise. 'Going back to acting has nothing to do with being famous or doing anything great. It's because there were so many resentments when I stopped. I want to pursue it as a growth for me. I'm looking for an agent. I really haven't done it in years. I haven't lost my hair and I'm not grey yet. I think it's more therapeutic for me than anything else. Instead of not doing it for resentment it's now a choice for me at least to perceive doing it on my own again, and not for anybody else – not because I have the pressure to raise a family or because someone thinks I need to do that. I feel if I don't give it a shot I will always be second-guessing. I want to make sure that it's not because I'm somebody's brother.'

He can expect little help from his sister Jodie. There's a hard edge to her character even where her own family is concerned. She shies away from anything that smacks of nepotism and expects other people, including her brothers and sisters, to stand on their own two feet. Buddy loyally defends her motives. 'Jodie doesn't want to feel that if there was a problem she would feel responsible. Our family doesn't work like that. My sister Jodie takes care of my mother solely. My sister is real against any kind of nepotism or helping us to get any work within the business. My sister Connie is an interior designer who wants to do set dressing and I've never seen her do any of that.'

These days his relationship with Jodie is affectionate, although they don't see a great deal of each other. 'I am very proud of her. We have had lunch together and talked. She would be the first to say that she was like my shadow when we were children.'

Buddy regrets the lost years when he grew apart from his sister.

In particular he regrets not getting in touch with her during the Hinckley episode. 'I never called her to say I was sorry about it. Of course it would be a different story now, but I was so miserable and self-obsessed then that I just never bothered.'

He has come to terms with his feelings towards his mother. Therapy has taught him to let go of his compulsion to make her admit publicly that he supported his family at a crucial time. 'I wish that we could have been closer, but maybe I was always wishing for something she couldn't do and that was just acknowledge that I did give up a part of my life that was important for me to help raise my family – my sisters and my mom.'

Letting go was a struggle which took years. Buddy kept on hoping his mother would thank him for his efforts. He would challenge her about it, and yet she still couldn't see how important it had become to him. Even now he talks about it carefully, unwilling to rake over the hurt.

Three years ago, however, she acknowledged that he had contributed. Jodie became the peacemaker. 'My sister Jodie told me that. She said she really appreciated what I had done and so did my mother. My mother and I have talked. I think sometimes she tries to understand, but maybe she doesn't want to admit it to herself. She obviously feels something because she gets very uncomfortable when we talk. I think part of her wants to and the other part of her doesn't want to consider that she has any part in it. But we have discussed it and I have never felt any closure on it with her. I stopped bringing those things up, and I learned through therapy that I have to move on with my life. Obviously we all have our choices and carry our baggage with us through life.'

He understands now that they will never be close, and is content to build up the relationship with his three children and not let that lapse like his own father did. 'My children live with their mothers, but I see a great deal of them. I raised Lucius until he was fifteen. Then he went to live with his mother because he didn't have a relationship with her – that was good, because he needed that time with her.

'If any of my children wanted to be a child actor I wouldn't allow them to do it. You're sheltered in an unreal world, and when you get into the real world it's a shock that you are not prepared for. You are pampered. Then it all changes and you get pimples and your looks go and you are suddenly an outcast.

'I hate to think what will happen to Macaulay Culkin – I don't think he can act yet. I feel sorry for the kid, especially when he hits puberty and gets ugly. When he gets older and can't earn the kind of money he has been earning, it will be painful.'

Looking back, Buddy thinks he can see now why Jodie's career flourished and his did not. In some ways it was a matter of temperament, but it also had to do with the luck of being born a girl.

'Being female is easier. You are more in touch emotionally, and Jodie has always been able to self-analyse. Most people are forever competing with their peer group. Jodie never felt the need to compete. She was smart enough to see that, when most of us average kids just didn't.'

He is concerned about other young actors like Macaulay Culkin who earn large sums of money early in their lives. He would like to see legal guidelines laid down to protect their earnings. 'Things are still not what they should be. The law says the money should be put away for the children, but parents can apply to the court to invest it in property, for example. And suddenly the kids grow up and find, like I did, that it's all gone. The laws need to be stricter.'

Talking to Buddy now, it is clear that he is a happy and fulfilled man. He feels his story is a positive one. He fought his demons and beat them. It could have ended in bitterness, disappointment and tragedy, but it didn't. Buddy too possesses a measure of the steel it has taken to drive his sister Jodie to the top.

He still has things to prove to himself. If he makes it as an adult actor it might not make him any happier, but even the attempt will settle the final ghosts in his own mind.

And if he doesn't . . . well, that's all right too.

FIVE

Obsession – John Hinckley

Film stars, politicians and indeed anybody to whom the mantle 'rich and famous' can be applied are at risk from the same insidious threat – that one day a loved one will be kidnapped and held at ransom for money or tortured and killed for political motive. There is also the fear of that other group of people, the mentally unbalanced or deranged, who focus their damaged minds on a single figure and set out to make a mark on the world by taking that person out of it. They are often life's losers, the socially inadequate loners who develop the conviction that one meaningful act will put them where they feel they belong – at the centre of attention.

On 30 March 1981 such a person – John Warnock Hinckley Jnr – shot and wounded President Ronald Reagan as he left a conference at the Washington Hilton Hotel. A bullet lodged in the President's left lung. White House Press Secretary James Brady was also shot and badly hurt. Brady suffered severe brain damage and after five operations emerged paralysed.

Over the next few days a bizarre link between the shooting and Jodie Foster emerged. Investigators who searched John Hinckley's motel room in Washington found letters to the actress and photographs of her. A profile of an isolated drifter unable to form substantial relationships with other people was gradually pieced together. The pattern of his life, and in particular his movements during the months prior to the shooting, made chilling reading, particularly for the young Yale student who had done her best to combine the life of a Hollywood film star with that of a university freshman.

She was, in her own words, 'skipping across the campus with my best friend' when someone yelled at her that Reagan had been shot. Her reaction on hearing that the would-be assassin was John Hinckley was one of stunned disbelief. He was the persistent admirer who had become such a nuisance and a worry that she had shown his ardent letters to her college dean, Eustace Theodore. Three weeks before the assassination attempt, he gave them to the campus police, who, together with police in New Haven, Connecticut, tried in vain to track down the writer of the notes to warn him off. The notes were, in fact, considered harmless, and as they did not break any law they were not seen as significant until after the President was shot.

On the surface Jodie was cool. Her actress's training took over and she delivered the performance of her life. It was the tough kid act she knew so well. Few saw her fear, her insecurity, her worry that there would be copycat attempts, other nutcases trying to get to her – as indeed there were. She kept it all to herself and a close circle of friends while the investigation proceeded.

On paper John Hinckley was an unlikely assassin. He was born into middle-class America on 29 May 1955 in Ardmore, Oklahoma, with all the advantages that wealthy parents could give him. His father, also John, now sixty-nine, was a successful oil engineer who later became president of the prosperous Vanderbilt Energy Company.

When John was three, the devoutly Christian family moved to Dallas where Mr Hinckley's increasingly profitable business took him. Young John, his brother Scott, now forty-six, and sister Diane, now forty-two, went to the prestigious Highland Park High School, favoured by wealthy families. It was the kind of school where academic excellence is expected and all-round achievers were turned out.

With the benefit of hindsight it is easy for friends and acquaintances to pinpoint the landmarks of change in Hinckley's personality – from being an active student who was his class president twice and a keen basketball and football player, to a more reserved and withdrawn adolescent who seemed to suffer in the shadow of a beautiful and talented sister and a clever and successful brother. He always felt he could not live up to people's expectations of him, and his withdrawal was gradual. A high school contemporary said at the time: 'If I saw him, I'd know him, but I wouldn't think or say, "That's John Hinckley," I would think, "That's Diane's brother." Everybody knew his sister real well, but not him.'

The lonely teenager would sit for hours in his bedroom practising the guitar and listening to rock and roll music. He graduated from high school in 1973 and headed for Texas Tech University in Lubbock. Meanwhile his father and mother, Jo-Ann, moved to Denver, Colorado, where Mr Hinckley relocated his business. Mr Hinckley senior was a staunch supporter of the Republican Party, and as his personal prosperity grew he contributed vast sums to election campaigns. He was a personal friend of former President George Bush, and the families socialized together.

Both Diane and Scott chose the conventional and accepted route through to adulthood. Diane, the lovely college cheerleader, became Diane the stunning bride who married Dallas insurance underwriter Stephen Sims. Scott went into his father's firm, where he became a vice-president. But while Scott Hinckley was a regular dinner guest at the Denver home of George Bush's son Neil, John's world became increasingly isolated from conventional social contact.

His studies were intermittent: he would break off and disappear for months on end. During his years at Texas Tech, seven in all, Hinckley's personality underwent considerable change. He developed an obsessive interest in Nazism. He chose Hitler's *Mein Kampf* as the subject of one history report and the concentration camp at Auschwitz as another, and got excellent marks for both – 90 per cent for the essay on *Mein Kampf*. In fact, his tutor, Professor Otto Nelson, remarked that it was the first time any student of his had actually read it. 'He did a good job,' he said.

Most of his other academic marks were fairly average – C grades rather than As. Professor Nelson remembers Hinckley as being a lot more isolated than the others. 'He sat by himself. He was usually two or three chairs from the other students.'

Around that time his taste in music became more extreme. He

would listen to punk records for hours, and lost touch with his old high-school friends one by one.

In April 1976 the seeds of another passion were planted with the opening in a Lubbock cinema of the film *Taxi Driver*, starring Robert de Niro and Jodie Foster. The story of the psychopath, played by de Niro, who stalks a political candidate fascinated Hinckley with its elaborate gun rituals. Foster played the teenage prostitute who befriended the lonely and obsessed assassin who wasted away his life in cheap hotels dreaming of the moment when the world would sit up and take notice of him.

Hinckley was mesmerized by de Niro's powerful performance and began to nurture the notion of death as the ultimate solution to crime and other life problems. He also fell in love with Jodie Foster, then a slim, childlike thirteen-year-old whose adolescent body had not yet caught up with her otherwise wordly air, and eyes that appeared to understand all.

One of his drop-out periods followed shortly afterwards, and he went to live in Hollywood for a while. There and in various student apartments back in Lubbock the pattern was the same. There never seemed to be any friends around, certainly no girlfriends. He would sit in his room and read and eat junk food, leaving the wrappers lying carelessly around the floor.

The nearest he got to social contact was with the proprietor of a second-hand book shop where he would browse among volumes on guns and Nazi Germany. Lonie Montgomery, the proprietor, said: 'He never said a word. He'd just go to those books on Germany and firearms and look them over for an hour at a time or even longer.'

Hinckley's involvement with Nazism became more intense, and in March 1978 he disappeared from college for several weeks. His father thought he had gone off with his guitar in pursuit of a musical career. But in fact he had travelled to Chicago to join the National Socialist Party of America – the US Nazi Party. He even took part in one of their 'storm trooper' rallies, but other members found him 'too extreme' and 'uncontrollable' and he was expelled from the party. 'He seemed more prone towards violence than most of our members,' said Michael C. Allen, a party leader who was disturbed by Hinckley's notion of murder as a solution to problems. 'He was a nut. He wanted to shoot people and blow things up,' said Allen. After the Nazis threw him out Hinckley joined a Los Angeles-based, even more extreme right-wing group called Posse Comitatis (Latin for Powers of the County), whose symbol is a hangman's noose and who see themselves as vigilantes whose duty it is to try, convict and sentence wrongdoers.

It is known that Hinckley's parents helped him to obtain psychiatric care in the year before the shooting, although it seems he was on medication prior to that, including the anti-depressant Valium. He was also experimenting with marijuana.

No one is quite sure when he developed his fascination with guns, but records from two pawn shops in Lubbock showed that he bought three handguns in September 1980, just when he should have been embarking on his final term at college. Instead he decided to drop out for the last time. He cleaned out his bank account and set out on a series of journeys which ended with his arrest in Washington.

But first there was an incident in Nashville which, on reflection, might have alerted the authorities to the possibility that this man was a threat to society. He was arrested at Nashville Metropolitan Airport for allegedly carrying guns in his luggage. Two .22 calibre revolvers, one .38 calibre handgun, fifty rounds of ammunition and a pair of handcuffs were discovered as they were put through an X-ray machine. President Carter was visiting Nashville at the time to speak at the Grand Ole Opry, but airport security men did not place any significance on that at the time and, after questioning, Hinckley was allowed to pay bond and court costs of $62.50 (about £30), and walk free.

Later Hinckley revealed in a series of letters to *New York Post* reporter George Carpozi Jnr that he had thought about killing President Carter. 'Why? I hated Carter. I hated myself. I was too chicken to commit suicide. I read a book about the Lindbergh kidnapping and thought about kidnapping someone myself. I read about John Dillinger and I thought about robbing banks. Do you get the picture?

'Some time in late June or July, Carter was in Dallas for a barbecue fundraiser. I planned to drive over to Big D and take a shot at Big C with a newly purchased .22 rifle with a great scope. The reason I didn't go to Dallas was because one of Jodie's movies was on TV the same night and I didn't want to miss it! I swear it!' wrote Hinckley, who started corresponding with the journalist after complaining of Carpozi's coverage of him in the *New York Post*.

Hinckley never turned up to answer the charges, but even that was not a surprising event in Nashville, where officials deal with four or five such cases every month.

Three days later he was in Dallas buying more guns, and by October he was in Denver applying for jobs, using fictitious qualifications including a claim that he studied at Yale.

He made several trips to New Haven, Connecticut, to be near the Yale campus, staying in cheap motels and eating at the nearby McDonald's. The strange young man stayed alone for sixteen days at the Golden Hours Motel dreaming of Jodie Foster, writing letters to her and eventually working up the courage to phone her in her college rooms. He hung around the campus until he discovered where she stayed and pushed a letter under the door of her room. Although he never actually met her, he convinced himself that there was a special bond between them.

Jodie Foster gets hundreds of letters every week, many of them from cranks. Hinckley's letters had a distinctly disturbing quality which worried her but, although she went to the college dean with them, she did not think they were sufficiently serious to make a complaint to the New Haven police.

'If you don't love me, I'm going to kill the President,' he wrote in one. The words 'I have killed the President' were in another. In a third he told her, 'I'm going to do it for you' and 'I will prove my love to you through a historic act.'

Ronald Reagan had been President of the United States for just over four months when Hinckley attempted his 'historic act'. After speaking to an audience of trade unionists in a Washington hotel he was walking back to his limousine, waving to onlookers, when

Hinckley pushed through to the front of the crowd and fired six shots from a .22 revolver at a distance of ten feet.

One bullet lodged in the President's chest, just three inches from his heart. Hinckley shot three other men – Jim Brady, the President's Press Secretary, a secret service agent and a policeman – before he was overpowered and pinned up against a wall.

The President was bundled into a limousine and whisked straight to a Washington hospital, where he was well enough to joke with his anxious wife, 'Honey, I forgot to duck.' As he was wheeled into the theatre for an operation to remove the bullet he told the anaesthetists: 'I hope you guys are Republicans.'

Two days before he shot the President Hinckley wrote the following letter to Jodie but never posted it. Police found it in his hotel room.

Dear Jody [sic],

There is a definite possibility that I will be killed in my attempt to get Reagan. It is for this very reason that I am writing to you this letter now.

As you well know by now I love you very much, the past seven months I have left you dozens of poems, letters and messages in the faint hope you would develop an interest in me.

Although we talked on the phone a couple of times, I never had the courage to simply approach you and introduce myself. Besides my shyness, I honestly did not wish to bother you with my constant presence. I know the many messages left at your door and in your mailbox were a nuisance, but I felt it was the most painless way for me to express my love for you.

I feel very good about the fact you at least know my name and how I feel about you. And by hanging around your dormitory, I've come to realize that I'm the topic of more than a little conversation, however full of ridicule it may be. At least you know that I'll always love you.

Jody, I would abandon this idea of getting Reagan in a second if I could only win your heart and live out the rest of my life with you, whether it be in total obscurity or whatever. I will

admit to you that the reason I'm going ahead with this attempt
now is because I just cannot wait any longer to impress you. I've
got to do something now to make you understand in no
uncertain terms that I am doing all of this for your sake.

Jody, I'm asking you to please look into your heart and at least
give me the chance with this historical [sic] deed to gain your
respect and love.

I love you forever.
John Hinckley.

Also in the room detectives found photographs of the actress and
newspaper cuttings, as well as a picture of John F. Kennedy's
assassin, Lee Harvey Oswald, holding a gun, and articles about
other assassinations. There were cuttings about John Lennon,
another Hinckley idol. And there were tapes made by Hinckley of
phone calls to Jodie shortly before he shot the President.

The tapes make no reference to President Reagan or to any act
of violence, and consist largely of requests that she allow him to
phone her again. At one point you can hear Jodie's room-mates
giggling in the background and she tells him: 'They're laughing at
you.' Then she turns to the girls and says: 'I should tell him I am
sitting here with a knife.'

Hinckley heard the remark and said: 'Well, I'm not dangerous.
I promise you that.'

Hinckley asked her: 'Can I call tomorrow night?' to which she
replied, 'That's fine.'

Hinckley: 'Will you be in?'
Jodie: 'Maybe.'
Hinckley: 'Will you talk?'
Foster: 'Sure.'
Hinckley: 'Well, you just changed your mind, see.'

It seems extraordinary that she even bothered to answer the
calls, but this was no sophisticated thirty-two-year-old. This was a
hesitant teenager, unsure of herself in a world away from Hollywood – just another student, however well known, living on a
campus. After all, that was the way she wanted it.

Later in the conversation she snapped: 'Oh God, oh seriously, this is really starting to bother me. Do you mind if I hang up?'

'Oh Jodie, please . . .' were the anguished final words from Hinckley.

The bizarre connection between President Reagan and Jodie in his troubled mind has never been fully explained – whether he believed that Reagan had somehow slighted her or obstructed her career, or whether he was simply the ultimate target.

Police braced themselves for copycat attempts, and sure enough a few weeks later another 'crazy' was apprehended on his way to Washington to shoot the President. Edward Richardson, a twenty-three-year-old out-of-work gardener, was arrested in a New York bus station with a .32 revolver in his pocket.

He had clearly modelled himself on Hinckley, following his footsteps to New Haven, Connecticut, to be near Jodie and even staying in the same motel. Like Hinckley, he left a letter in his room explaining his intentions and protesting his love for Jodie. Luckily a maid found the letter and gave it to the police, who picked him up on his way from New Haven to Washington. The bearded young man from Drexel Hill, a fashionable suburb of Philadelphia, claimed that Hinckley had appeared to him in a dream, urging him to finish off the job by shooting the President. A note delivered to Jodie Foster's quarters at Yale threatened both her life and that of the President. Richardson was released into the community after a year in jail.

Before the trial psychiatrists spent months painstakingly trying to assess John Hinckley. His parents sent messages of sympathy to the victims while standing by their son. They hired the top Washington firm of Williams and Connolly to defend him and asked people to pray for him.

In a statement they said: 'We simply ask that you realize John is a sick boy and that you give him the benefit of the doubt until all the true facts concerning his mental condition are known.'

Hinckley himself wrote a letter to *Time* magazine's Washington correspondent, Evan Thomas, about his feelings for Jodie Foster, as if to prove his slippery grip on reality: 'The most important thing in my life is Jodie Foster's love and admiration. If I can't have them, neither can anybody else. We are a historical couple, like Napoleon and Josephine, and a romantic couple like Romeo and Juliet.'

During the trial, defence lawyers focused on Hinckley's obsession and the 'inner world' to which he retreated after Jodie Foster gave him the brush-off during several phone calls that he made to her at Yale. It was, they said, a tremendous blow to his self-esteem. Witnesses attested to his social inadequacies. He was an errant child, an isolated little boy and a totally ineffectual adult, they told the court. One defence witness said he was 'totally abnormal, suffering from a severe mental illness called schizophrenia spectrum disorder'. Another put it more simply, describing him as 'a classical nut'.

During the trial, which lasted eight weeks, Hinckley sat impassively in the dock of courtroom 19 of Washington's Federal District Court, pink-cheeked and wearing neat three-piece suits. Most of the time he just stared into space, but occasionally he laughed when some of his writings were read out. One piece was a poem he had written:

This mind of mine doesn't mind much of anything.
Unless it comes to mind
That I am out of my mind.

The only time he reacted angrily was when Jodie Foster's videoed testimony was shown, in which she said she did not know him.

In the back of the court his parents wept quietly at times, the very picture of suburban respectability, and they accepted the blame for what their son did because they had tried to make him stand on his own two feet and forced him to leave home. The court heard how Jack Hinckley wanted to take 'a strict authoritarian approach', while Jo-Ann favoured 'a permissive, protective stance'.

The trial was estimated to have cost more than $3 million. Defence and prosecution costs alone were estimated at around $1 million each, and a further $1 million was spent on the police and security men whose job it was to guard Hinckley while he was awaiting trial. One psychiatrist billed the government for almost $120,000 – one thousand hours at $120 an hour.

America followed the proceedings with fascination and Jodie became the unwilling focus of their interest. The validity of the plea of insanity provoked widespread debate. Both sides enrolled top psychiatrists to try to prove their points. It was, according to Alan Stone, a former president of the American Psychiatric Association, like 'clowns performing in a three-ring circus'.

The insanity plea was the only possible defence in view of the number of witnesses, the television footage and the evidence that Hinckley had planned the attack, bought special bullets and tracked the President to the Washington Hilton. The defence projected Hinckley as a teenage failure. Psychiatrist Dr William Carpenter of the University of Maryland, who interviewed him for forty-five hours, described him as a 'process schizophrenic'.

Dr Carpenter traced Hinckley's problems back to his adolescence, when he had been withdrawn and had no friends and begun to invent make-believe characters and eventually to believe his own fantasies. He was also obsessed with the music of John Lennon and after Lennon's death described himself as in total despair, his mind full of thoughts of murder, suicide and the end of the world.

His slide towards madness was accelerated by the sense of alienation he felt at home in the midst of a family of high achievers. His parents did not understand him and did not know how to help. They sent him to a Colorado psychiatrist, who prescribed Valium and suggested that his parents should take a firm line with him. Three weeks before the assassination attempt his father gave him $200 and told him to leave home. 'It was the greatest mistake of my life,' said Mr Hinckley senior.

Hinckley's psychiatrist, Dr John Hopper, said that in November 1980 his patient had told him he had two obsessions in his life – Jodie Foster and writing. 'I care about nothing else,' Hinckley told his doctor. Between 28 October 1980 and 27 February 1981 they had twelve therapy sessions, during which Hinckley spoke of the pressure of being the least successful person in a family of successful people. He did not feel confident or successful in relation to girls.

Disney signed Jodie up for her first full-length feature film at the age of eight – her co-star in *Napoleon and Samantha* was a 550 lb lion.

Reviews for this musical version of *Tom Sawyer* revealed Jodie as an actress with means beyond her years.

In spite of the maturity required from her profession, Jodie never lost the ability to relax like normal children of her own age.

Jodie was only fourteen when both *Bugsy Malone* and *Taxi Driver* were released (*above left and right*), but she demonstrated the same professional skill and sassy self-confidence as was evident four years later with *Carny* (*left*).

By comparison to the siren look of *Taxi Driver*, dressed in a bikini for *Il Cosotto* and
posing on her bike in *Candleshoe* a year later, Jodie appears merely childlike.
Below right: In her favourite cap.

Above left: Jodie's brother, Buddy, as a young boy in the days of *Mayberry RFD.*
Above right: Buddy today.

Below: Jodie with her mother, Brandy.

Above: With her close friends Rob Lowe and Nastassia
Kinski during filming of *Hotel New Hampshire.*
Right: During rehearsals for *Getting Out* at Yale.

Below left: John Hinckley.
Below right: Edward Richardson.

Above: The Accused – which led to Jodie's first Oscar.

Below: Winning her second Oscar with Sir Anthony Hopkins for
The Silence of the Lambs.

Above: Jodie's first taste of directing came with *Little Man Tate*, starring Adam Hann-Byrd and herself.

Below left: Sommersby.
Below right: Maverick.

Above left : Jodie relaxing with Marco Pasanella, her old friend from Yale . . .
. . . and with Randy Stone (*above right*).
Below: Jodie the enigma.

Dr Hopper said he had advised Hinckley's parents to force their son to make it on his own and devised a rigid plan of rules and deadlines to help them cope with him.

Other evidence of the fantasy love affair Hinckley carried on included a card to Jodie, never posted, expressing the hope that one day he and she would occupy the White House together like President Reagan and his wife Nancy:

> Dear Jodie,
>   Don't they make a darling couple? Nancy is downright sexy. One day you and I will occupy the White House and the peasants will drool with envy. Until then please do remain a virgin. You are a virgin, aren't you?

Paperbacks seized by the FBI included *The Fan*, the story of a deranged man who stalks an actress, *Taxi Driver*, the book of the film, and *The Fox Is Crazy Too*, about a criminal who escapes the law by feigning insanity.

In his writings, Hinckley portrays himself as psychologically bruised beyond hope. 'I can't begin to be happy, regardless of your dream come true I continue to grovel for normalcy, I continue to scream inside. I stagger from day to day. I stagger toward the future. Regardless of the laughter of children, I cannot continue to pretend. I cannot continue to live.'

For every expert whom the defence produced, the prosecution brought in another who disagreed. Dr Park Dietz, a Harvard psychiatrist, suggested that the assassination attempt was an easy for Hinckley to achieve the fame he was unwilling to work for. He was not psychotic and had never lost touch with his own identity.

In his summing up, Judge Barrington Parker explained that under the law the jury must return a verdict of not guilty by reason of insanity if they decided that, as a result of mental disease or defect, Hinckley 'lacked the substantial capacity either to conform his conduct to the law or to appreciate the wrongfulness of his conduct'. He reminded the jury that the burden was on the state to prove that Hinckley was sane beyond reasonable doubt.

After twenty-four hours of deliberation the jury returned the verdict that John Hinckley was not guilty because of insanity of attempting to assassinate President Reagan. It caused uproar and led to demands for a change in American law. Jodie Foster was horrified. She knew that if he was ever released she would never have peace of mind again. If he was capable of shooting the President of the United States, who has $60 million worth of security around him, he could get to her too. The fact that he was in a secure mental hospital gave her little comfort. Clearly his obsession with her was as strong as ever, and over the next few years she was to be faced with more evidence of it.

In August 1982, the back issues department of the American magazine *High Society* was stunned to receive a handwritten request from Hinckley, enclosing a cheque for $5, for the March 1982 issue of the magazine, which contained sexy pictures of Jodie. They were unsure whether to comply or not and eventually compromised by sending a copy to Hinckley's doctors at St Elizabeth's Hospital, Washington, leaving it up to them whether or not to pass it on.

He also wrote rambling notes and poems to various publications, including the *National Enquirer*. The poems that he wrote were violent and upsetting. One, addressed to Jodie and published in that magazine, contains these vicious lines: 'I have come to shoot you down with my bloody gun . . . look here at my bloody knife, I think I'll stab you first, deep into your bloody heart, it should quench my thirst.' Foster was furious that the magazine had published it and asked the Justice Department to prosecute. Her lawyers called the August 1982 edition of the magazine a 'threat to Miss Foster that violated federal law'. Lawyer Jonathan Sallet said: 'It's illegal to help Hinckley threaten Miss Foster and it doesn't make any difference whether it's a private person or a newspaper who gives him this aid. We want to stop these kinds of threats from being publicly disseminated.'

But the Justice Department decided not to prosecute, and declined to give a reason for the decision. Sources said it was felt that the case raised the issue of freedom of the press, which would probably make any prosecution fruitless.

Hinckley is being held at St Elizabeth's, a secure mental hospital, where he will stay until doctors decide, if ever, that he is normal. In theory, at least, he could one day be a free man again. 'The goal is eventually to move the person into the community. The criterion is that the person would not pose a danger,' said Dr Thomas Polly, Director of the In-Patients Bureau.

Dr Polly would only talk in general terms about his patients and not specifically about John Hinckley. 'All patients are committed as in-patients. They can progress from maximum to minimum security and then to out-patients. Whenever the hospital feels that the patient is ready, they can petition the courts. It's a graduated process which combines clinical assessment with other factors. There would be a full public hearing before a judge.'

In Hinckley's case there has been no petition so far. He is committed to being an in-patient indefinitely at the 271-bed hospital set in extensive grounds and surrounded by a ten-feet-high chained fence. Some of the buildings date back to the Civil War, giving the place a university campus feel. As they progress, patients are allowed increased access to the grounds unescorted, as a precursor to community placement. They wear their own clothes and have their own rooms with television, radio and books.

Dr Polly denied a story in an American tabloid that John Hinckley had married, but he still attracts attention from disturbed people who feel an affinity with him. In 1984 a nineteen-year-old college student, Penny Bailey, who was charged with threatening the life of an ex-teacher of hers, admitted writing to Hinckley offering to kill Jodie Foster. Bailey, a student at Daley Junior College, Chicago, felt herself a kindred spirit of Hinckley and in a letter compared her 'love–hate relationship' with her high-school teacher to Hinckley's infatuation with Foster. 'You are not alone in your quest to find that one very special person that you are willing to die for or be killed for,' she wrote.

A letter he wrote back to her was later used by federal prosecutors to block his request for a visit to his family. In 1987 Hinckley applied for leave to visit his family at Easter, and Judge Barrington Parker was once again asked to make a judgement on his state of mind after a psychiatrist testified that Hinckley had given up his obsession with Foster. But when the judge ordered a search of his room, it revealed twenty photographs of Jodie and notes and writings which made it clear that he had not. The court also heard that Hinckley had exchanged letters with triple murderer Theodore Bundy, who was then on Death Row but has since been executed.

In his letter to Penny Bailey he outlined three courses of action – mail him a .38 calibre pistol so he could escape from St Elizabeth's, take the bus to New Haven to kill Foster, or hijack an aeroplane from Chicago to Washington's National Airport where she was to demand that Hinckley and Foster be brought to the airport.

Doctors say Hinckley still suffers from complicated and serious mental disorders characterized by 'magical thinking' and bizarre fantasies, including a belief that Miss Foster secretly admires him. His lawyer, Vincent J. Fuller, told me: 'There is no doubt that he was severely disturbed. Had it been anybody other than the President of the United States of America, the government would have concluded that he was insane and there would have been no trial. But because it was the President there had to be a show trial. His mental condition is reviewed every year, and there is a possibility that he might one day get out.'

Mr Fuller, who met Jodie on several occasions during the weeks leading up to the trial, said of her: 'She was extraordinarily courteous and polite, but I think she was quite distraught that she was dragged into this thing by what he had done.'

SIX

Tough Kid

The lasting effect on Jodie Foster of the John Hinckley affair is hard to imagine. She appears finally to have left it behind her although for a long time it hurt her deeply.

She drew on all her resources as an actress, however, and presented a serene face to the world even though inside she was anguished. She called it 'playing cowboy', a reference to the tough kid act she put on for everybody else's benefit.

The shock of those first terrible hours was profound and the effect rippled through her life for years to come. When she first heard that the President had been shot it didn't even cross her mind that there could have been any connection with herself or with the young man who had been pestering her with his unwelcome attentions in the form of letters and phone calls.

World events hardly touched the group she moved around with. They were more interested in steeping themselves in the past than the present and maintained a lofty distance from life outside college. It was a cosy academic life cushioned from reality, which is one reason why the news that Reagan's assailant was her admirer John Hinckley hit her so hard.

The Dean of the Faculty did his best to cushion the blow as he told her that pictures of her, and her college address, had been found in Hinckley's room. Her college lecturers tried to be kind but they didn't really know how to treat her. Nothing like this had pierced their cloistered academic world before.

Even with her closest friends Jodie did not know whether to laugh or to cry. She did both and the pain was almost unbearable.

'My body jerked in painful convulsions. I hurt. I was no longer thinking of the President, of the assailant, of the crime, of the press. I was crying for myself. Me, the unwilling victim. The one who would pay in the end. The one who paid all along – and, yes, keeps paying,' she wrote in an article for *Esquire* magazine twenty months later.

It was an extraordinarily emotional outpouring from someone unused to exposing her inner feelings publicly and it expressed eloquently the turmoil she went through. Jodie revealed more about herself then than she ever gave away before or since.

A few years ago she purchased the copyright of the article from *Esquire* so it is not possible to reproduce it, which is a pity because the quality of the writing displays an incisive and analytical mind and a perceptiveness of her own and other people's motives and behaviour that would do credit to a trained psychologist.

The fact that she felt it necessary to buy the rights to the piece, extracts from which have been published in newspapers and magazines all over the world, reveals a determination to have control over her own life and as far as possible banish all thoughts of John Hinckley from it.

She was persuaded to write the piece by *Esquire*'s former editor Lee Eisenberg, forty-six, who later offered the young actress summer work on the magazine and became a friend and confidant. In fact she did not need much persuading to write down her feelings. She had read so much rubbish about what happened that she felt she wanted to tell the story from her point of view and in her own words. Also, she had written for Eisenberg before she went to college and trusted him to reproduce her work faithfully, which he did.

Eisenberg, now out of journalism altogether and working on a development programme of schools management called The Eddison Project, is protective of her in a way that is typical of many of her friends.

She and I have been friends for a very long time. Most of what she went through she has written about herself and I guess that's all she wants to say about it. She has unwittingly found herself on some difficult situations but she hasn't stirred that pot.

She is unlike any other celebrities. She has been constant from the beginning and has largely let her work speak for herself. She isn't as hypocritical as many in the business. She has earned the loyalty of her friends consistent with the way she has chosen to live her life.

As a piece of writing, the lengthy *Esquire* article is meticulously punctuated, accurately phrased, an exercise in perfectionism in itself. Jodie digs right down in a one-off insight into the depths of despair into which she sank.

Sometimes the strain of hiding her feelings became almost intolerable. 'That kind of pain doesn't go away. It's something you never understand, forgive or forget. It is a pain that can never be healed with a kiss from your mother's lips or a "ssh, everything's OK". Everying's not OK! It's not,' she wrote.

It was typical of Jodie that she demanded control of the story which made world news. If anyone was going to tell it accurately from her point of view, it was going to be her. Her writing was honest and colourful, sometimes self-indulgent and perhaps in later years she may have regretted being so forthcoming.

An older, wiser Jodie might not have exhibited such a gigantic, soaring and wounded ego, an overwhelming feeling of superiority and a compulsion to win. There is also evidence of a tender and vulnerable character who yearned to be loved and appreciated for herself as well as her talent and intelligence, which after all is inseparable from the whole.

Her desire to fit in was overwhelming, which is part of the reason she was so distraught by the unwelcome attention Hinckley's mad attempt to impress her brought her. Writing about the pain of her experiences served as a catharsis for Jodie, a purging of the bitter emotions which swamped and confused her. She needed to put down on paper what she was thinking in order to recognize and assess her true feelings and after that she filed it neatly away, publicly at any rate, and did her best to avoid answering any more questions on the subject of John Hinckley for a very long time.

Here was a young woman struggling to regain control over her life after a bizarre event over which she had none but which nevertheless threatened to engulf her. It was a time in her life when writing came easily. Her language was flowery and extravagant and at times a jumble of emotions tumbled onto the page full of a young woman's need to be loved and appreciated.

After all the effort she had made to fit in with the student world, she was bitter that she had been singled out for attention in such extraordinary circumstances. She had worked her way through the insecurities she had about being different from the rest in that she knew she had a job to go to at the end of her studies and they didn't. She felt she had been accepted by the student population for what she was. The Hinckley affair put her back to square one in that respect.

Now, once again, Jodie felt the need to put on a good show, to be tough and show the world that she was strong. She thought she had managed to perpetuate the image that she had so assiduously created of a normal, well-adjusted girl who could not be tipped off balance. She almost convinced herself that it was true and drew upon strength that she did not know she had.

The tough kid act was, after all, what she had been portraying on screen since she was ten years old. Perhaps it was nearer to her real persona than she had realized. Like the characters she had played, Jodie felt an overwhelming compulsion to survive this life trauma and not go under either mentally or physically. It stood her in good stead because she soon realized that if she did not get a grip of her life, nobody else was going to.

She started making her own enquiries in an effort to work her way through the most unusual situation she was ever to find herself in. All the time, information was being leaked to the press and Jodie found herself reading the newspapers and listening to the local news on the radio in order to piece together what was happening.

One of the most frightening aspects of the whole experience was the media. As a child star she had handled hundreds of press interviews with aplomb but this was different. She was not willingly publicizing some new movie, she was an unwilling part of a major story and people wanted to know everything about her at a time when all she wanted was to be anonymous.

She decided to meet that particular problem head on by organizing her own press conference and reading a statement she had written herself against all the advice from officialdom. She just wanted to get it over with quickly so that she could retreat once again into her student world.

Her analytical mind could see that she was just a story to the press men and women and she tried hard not to take their prurient interest personally. She was determined that they were not to be permitted to destroy her life but at the same time she knew she would be the object of fascination to them for a very long time. She even felt sorry for them.

She felt that by giving a press conference and lifting the curtain a little on her inner feelings she would be embarking on a sort of deal with them. She would tell them how shocked and frightened she had been and in return she would be left alone. Or at least that was the plan. She told reporters: 'I felt very sad, frightened, distressed. I acted badly. I guess I cried.'

At the same time she was anxious not to make the connection between Hinckley and *Taxi Driver* even though she had been told that her part in the film was what triggered his obsession. 'I'm not here to answer questions about *Taxi Driver*. In no way have I ever been sorry about any film I have done.'

After it was over Jodie began to feel very much alone. Everyone had been kind to her, but none of it helped.

She decided she must simply knuckle down and get back to student life. People did their best not to show interest and some of her friends even deliberately ignored her in order to give her space. She felt split in two. There were two Jodie Fosters. The one up on the screen with her blonde hair and bright smile and the other one which only she knew, 'shrouded in bravado and wit but, underneath, a creature crippled, without self-esteem, a frail and alienated being'.

But she forced herself to go to classes and pretend it hadn't happened. She did not want to be different, 'a returning war hero to be paraded'. Above all she did not want to be seen as a victim. She cut herself off from all but a few close friends and probably did not even realize how badly she had been affected by what had happened. Jodie had changed for ever but she did not know it.

Time and again she would ask herself why John Hinckley had developed an obsession with her, but she couldn't answer that and it made her even more confused. What upset her even more was the knowledge that people who she thought were her friends talked to the press. She felt betrayed and once again isolated. It was clear to her that, try as she may, she was still something of an outsider, different, and she hated that.

To outsiders Jodie's tough kid act worked fairly well until another incident shook her to the core.

A second man – Edward Richardson from Pennsylvania – was arrested in New York carrying a loaded gun, hoping to finish off the job John Hinckley failed to do and kill the President. He too claimed to be obsessed with Jodie Foster and admitted that he had gone to New Haven with the intention of killing her but decided she was too pretty and he couldn't go through with it.

Jodie realized that he was the same bearded man she had noticed in the audience one night during a performance of a college play in which she had a major role. She had been distracted by the shutter of a camera and noticed him sitting there staring at her. Police who had been working to track down the writer of a death-threat note had caught up with Richardson as he boarded a bus from New Haven and followed him discreetly to New York.

The knowledge that she had been within ten feet of a madman with a loaded gun who had thought about killing her was devastating. Finally the full trauma of the events of the past month hit her like an avalanche.

For the first time she began to question the validity of her own actions, wondering why she had forced herself to carry on with the play, for example, when people would have understood had she pulled out.

One of her friends was quoted as saying: 'Jodie thought that maybe she should back out, but without her the play would have had to be cancelled. She just decided that she had to prove to the world that she wasn't going to let Hinckley run her life.'

All that bravado seemed suddenly pointless to her, ridiculous. She had practically stared death in the bearded face and for what? It was the beginning of a nightmare period of fear and apprehension that cut deep into Jodie's confidence and has never altogether left her. Her own description is graphic and vivid. You can almost smell her fear. She began to see death everywhere. Being photographed felt like being shot and she admitted that it still did.

> I thought everyone was looking at me in crowds; perhaps they were. Every sick letter I received I made sure to read, to laugh at, to read again. People were punishing me because I was there. They were hurting me intentionally without any physical contact. They were manifesting a need to wound and I just happened to be the victim.

Her words are dramatic and harsh and they present a blindingly obvious reason for the actress's near-paranoia about privacy, her secrecy and her desire to let her work speak for itself and her private life remain private. Still, she stuck it out till the end of her freshman year in May 1981, when she packed up her things and returned to Los Angeles and a hiking holiday in the hills.

In the autumn she went back to college and began to feel that things were getting back to normal. She avoided having her photograph taken because of the extra pounds she had piled on, but on the rare occasions when she would be snapped leaving a restaurant, for example, she would grin bravely as if she hadn't a care in the world.

But somehow her studies alone were not enough. She was getting restless. She needed to work, to get back into the world of movie-making where she felt comfortable and safe.

Then she was sent a script which appealed to her and would take her off to Manhattan to star in a movie with Peter O'Toole. It was an opportunity to escape for a while and Jodie began to believe there might be light at the end of the tunnel she found herself in.

There was still the trial to come, however, and she knew she would be thrust back into the unwelcome spotlight. Bravely she steeled herself for the ordeal but it was a time of heavy introspection when she examined the purpose of her life as an actress and the effect of the words she used in films on the people who watched her movies.

'I raise my eyebrows, you think I'm sexy. I dart my eyes, you think I'm smart. Actors and non-actors all manipulate. An actor simply has more personalities and techniques to draw on. And more people to manipulate.'

She took a brutally honest look at her craft and even began to search for evidence of her own responsibility for Hinckley's actions. It is part of Jodie Foster's nature to accept responsibility and she was gradually coming to a conclusion at this time in which she partly accepted this responsibility although she ultimately rejected it.

'So of course Hinckley "knew" me. That woman on the screen was digging in her bag of tricks and representing herself for everyone to assess, to get to know, to take home.'

It was as if she needed to set out on a journey of self-discovery in order to understand why these events had happened and she did it by writing it down. Some days would be worse than others and as time went by the gaps between the bad days would widen, but then something would happen to bring it all flooding back. To begin with she would politely decline to talk about it 'because every time it's in the press it just brings someone back to shoot at me'.

Occasionally, however, she would bring the subject up with a journalist who had been warned not to talk about it by publicists and by Jodie's mother. In 1983 it was reported that Hinckley claimed he was totally recovered. She said:

I don't think he'll ever get out. It would just cause too much controversy and they would have to change the law regarding the insanity plea. The cons for that are very strong. The truth is that only three per cent of all violent or homicidal felons ever use insanity. The reason is because it's expensive and long. I mean, nobody has a million dollars to spend on their trial.

He had a trust fund. But they figured it out in such a way that if someone were to sue him, he doesn't have any money. I would love to have sued him. I spent so much money for something I had nothing to do with.

The composed reply certainly did not sound like the woman who wrote the 'Why Me?' article.

Three years on she was saying: 'It's over. I don't think anyone cares any more and if they do it's just too bad. It's the one thing I don't like to comment on because unfortunately it just brings me back into target practice.'

She was clearly still shaky about the experience. 'I went crazy for a while and although the movie camera is my best friend, my buddy, I am still paranoid about having a picture taken on the street. It is also advantageous that I choose to play varying roles in different costumes and wigs. I do not cultivate a single Jodie Foster image,' she said.

'I never go into shops. It's a terrible thing for a woman to say but I hate shopping. It makes me nervous. My mom does my shopping. I truly come alive when I am in the safe bosom of my other family, a forty-five-person film crew.'

Ten years after that she admitted to a certain amount of embarrassment at the passionate outpouring. 'When I think back on it I feel like a real idiot. It's so emotional. But I was eighteen. You know what it says without me even knowing? It makes a comment on a paranoid thing of me always thinking I'm responsible,' she said.

That was the grown-up Jodie rationalizing it in her own mind. As the years went on she became less patient with her questioners and would freeze reporters who brought the subject of Hinckley up and refuse invitations to appear on television if she thought she was going to be asked about it.

Even as recently as 1991 she cancelled an interview with NBC's

Today show when she was told that John Hinckley's name would be mentioned in her introduction although they probably would not question her about it.

The questions simply refused to go away, however. She came to expect them when, for example, she portrayed a victim like Sarah Tobias in *The Accused* on screen, although her publicists did their best to ward them off and still do. Occasionally she comments a trifle abruptly: 'I can't stop playing a victim just because of Hinckley,' she told one interviewer. 'People don't want you to forget.'

The Silence of the Lambs raised the spectre of Hinckley once again with Jodie's portrayal of agent Clarice Starling on the trail of a vicious serial killer. 'I never thought of the script in terms of Hinckley until three weeks into shooting. I don't know why. Maybe I was blocking it.'

Jodie's formidable self-control and intelligence have forced the fears and insecurities into the background. She dealt with them gradually, plunging herself into the world she knows best, the world of film-making in which she grew up and which makes her feel secure. She relished the opportunity to play different roles, to change her appearance.

Her brother Buddy believes the experience changed Jodie permanently although the scars no longer show. 'I felt really bad for Jodie. I know she was really upset by it. I think it has had a long-term effect. She still gets scared sometimes. That's probably why you don't see much of her out and about. I suppose it's the price of stardom.'

Today's poised and calm woman knows she cannot change the past and she has stopped blaming herself. 'I had no responsibility for what happened. I want people to see my films, to be interested in me as an actress.'

Yet even though on the one hand she is not to blame for the assassination attempt on President Reagan, she is also aware that some kind of inner strength in her attracted Hinckley's interest. Somehow he knew that she could take a lot of pressure. 'Yeah, I was the right person,' she told an interviewer, meaning that somebody else might not have withstood it. 'This bravado thing was and still is a big part of my life. In general, I felt it was my God-given responsibility to endure this martyrdom and it's a good thing I went through it because somebody else couldn't take it.'

Even if dark doubts and fears do still cast a shadow across her mind she would never voice them out loud. That would be admitting that Hinckley had some sort of hold over her.

He doesn't.

He's a loser and she, most definitely, is not.

SEVEN

Yale – Foster the Student

Back in April 1980 Jodie had just one thing on her mind –
university. Like thousands of other high-school graduates
she spent the month waiting for the envelopes to drop
through her letter box informing her that she had won a place at
the college of her choice.

She needn't have worried. Having graduated from the Lycée
with honours, top of her class, she virtually had her pick of places.
In fact six top universities offered her places – Yale, Harvard,
Princeton, Columbia, Berkeley and Stanford. She fell in love with
Yale, partly because of the ivy-clad beauty of the campus at New
Haven, Connecticut, but also because it is only eighty-five miles
from New York. Coincidentally, Yale was her father's alma mater
and his father's before him, although that had little to do with her
decision to go there.

Jodie had just finished *Carny*, her fifteenth feature film, and
with one Academy nomination in the bag she was a sought-after
young actress. Her decision to turn her back on Hollywood to spend
several years studying stunned producers and publicists alike.

Film-making, however, was to her a job. Spending time enriching her mind in an academic life was an experience she was
determined to have. She wanted to be a normal student, to live that
self-indulgent and stimulating life, to give herself a chance to grow
up with young men and women from all walks of life who had
nothing to do with the movie world.

Los Angeles was fun. She grew up there. But she always felt it
didn't stretch her intellectually. 'If you've grown up there you
realize how silly it is and you love it for that. It's a fun place. You

don't talk to people. You go to the beach. All my life I figured if something's bothering you, you did things – you went to the gym, or driving in your car. But you never sat down and talked to anybody about anything.'

What she needed now was to learn to communicate with other people on an intellectual level, especially with people her own age. Most of all she wanted to measure herself by their standards, to see if she was as intelligent as her press agents were always telling journalists she was. She could recite the litany of her own exceptional gifts – the child who taught herself to read at three, whose favourite authors were André Malraux and James Joyce, the teenager who spoke fluent French and had a working knowledge of Italian and Spanish, the straight A student. At Yale she knew she would be only one of many who achieved straight As.

'It is the first time I've ever been around only people my own age. They were so brilliant, so special, the cream of American students. And everyone talks so fast. That's what I want.'

She wanted to immerse herself in literature, to expand her own writing skills, to join clubs, to belong to a group of friends with similar interests. There was so much hope in her heart that summer as she looked forward to Yale. 'I wanted an Ivy League education that was totally ivory towerish, not history and dates, but criticism. College was basically like strengthening a muscle, training my brain so that I could read and analyse and understand.'

If she could have just become another anonymous student she would have been happy. 'If people would look right through me. If three of us would go to a restaurant and they take us to a table for two,' she said.

With mock-Gothic spires and ivied courtyards, Yale was exactly what she imagined a college campus to be like. 'Yale actually invited me – little smog-ridden me – to sink my blond teeth into its dusty brick and ivy, I'm trading my life-guard shades for that good ol' New Haven Grime,' she wrote in an article for *Esquire* magazine just before her first term at college.

In her usual self-deprecating way she was making fun of the Hollywood-brat upbringing and showing admirable respect for the

Ivy League institution she had joined, hence the 'blond teeth', a slightly studenty metaphor for the California ethic.

Armed with an Olympia electric portable typewriter, a reading lamp, a suitcase full of 'preppie' clothes – the almost regulation Lacoste shirts and jeans – and without any of the trappings of the Hollywood film star, Jodie headed out East to Connecticut.

She felt a mixture of excitement about the prospect of such a completely different life and apprehension about a world of which she knew nothing. She was slightly nervous about meeting what she assumed would be sophisticated east coast students who had all been to private schools and had holiday homes in the fashionable Martha's Vineyard.

Most of all she was frightened that she wouldn't fit in. While she was full of confidence back home in Hollywood – she could walk into the smart Polo Lounge for a meeting with producers without batting an eyelid – the academic world was still foreign to her and she desperately wanted to be accepted for herself. She wondered if she would pass muster.

She was allocated a place in a dormitory in Welsh Hall on Yale's old campus, which she shared with three other girls, randomly selected. She settled down to begin lectures.

Yalies, as they are called, did their best to be unexcited about having a star in their midst. It was considered very uncool to be interested in her life and to a large extent Jodie was left to get on with it by her fellow students.

But even the sophisticated Yalies liked to gossip and a fund of Jodie Foster stories was passed around to eager listeners. Once over breakfast one student ticked off another over the pronunciation of German sociologist Max Weber's name.

'It's Vayber, not Weber.'

Jodie was unimpressed. 'You really shouldn't do that at breakfast,' she said.

Naturally reserved, if not secretive, she suddenly found that she loved the feeling of comradeship, the small talk with girlfriends, the giggling over boys. She was overheard enthusing about exchanging confidences. 'Why am I telling you all these things? I never tell anyone these things.' Her new friends were generally protective about her towards outsiders, especially the journalists who descended upon New Haven even before the Hinckley incident.

Jodie slopped around in jeans and tennis shoes with no make-up, doing her best not to draw attention to herself. In fact some of her male contemporaries were somewhat disappointed. The young men saw her as more of an 'intellectual' than a party girl, a little intimidating to all but her close friends.

She had been around Hollywood for long enough to separate the men who wanted to be seen with her because she was famous from the ones who were genuinely interested in her. It was easy for her to adopt a tough exterior and only allow those she chose really to get to know her.

Years later, back in her other world, she spoke of them with a certain wistfulness for a life that she could never regain. 'When I was at Yale I met some real nice cool guys who were wonderful to be around. They were a different breed and I miss that.'

Like most first-year students she would reinvent herself every few months as she tentatively explored the different groups of people that make up every university. One week she would be the theatre-type, next she would be into politics. Then it would be lengthy discussions in the small hours about literature and the meaning of life. 'The last year was smoking lots of cigarettes and wearing black. There was a lot of doing nothing. Having barbecues in my apartment.'

To begin with she tried to join all the clubs and societies she could possibly join, partly in an effort to win the approval of her fellow students. She went to college dances, football games, debates, everything – just to prove to them that she wasn't a stuck-up actress, that she was normal like them.

It took her a long time to relax and get to know that it was perfectly acceptable to be different, to realize she could actually be herself and still be liked. 'Being understood is not the most essential thing in life,' she wrote. But at the beginning it was difficult for her and all she wanted to do was conform.

For the university fresher, conforming actually means trying to

be thoroughly different by adopting outlandish modes of dress. It's
a 'screw-the-world' sort of attitude, a desire to make a statement,
to be noticed as somebody interesting. As with every other student
who has been through this phase, Jodie thought herself unique at
the time.

It was a wild, exciting period of her life when she experimented
with alcohol. She had a nasty bout with tequila and a thumping
hangover made her realize she did not want to repeat it. She
behaved in that harmless but irresponsible way which students like
to do – making mistakes without fear and enjoying letting her self-
imposed control over herself slip a little. Life was fun and to cap it
all she found she had actually grown in height and now measured
five feet four inches. She was elated.

She also enjoyed the learning process, going to lectures,
researching in libraries. 'I'm the kind of student who writes papers
a week in advance and never misses a single class. What I really
love about school is that it's incredibly abstract and intellectual. I
never took architecture or art or things like that because I can do
that on the outside. What I really need is something that's abstract,
that only exists on paper.

'My concentration at school was a lot better because I don't
have those job worries. I don't have to show my grades to my
parents. Also, I'm at school because I want to be, not because
anyone said, "You have to go", or because my parents went.'

She was not afraid of experimenting with style rather than
handing in an essay constructed 'by the book'. Sometimes her
tutors were forced to restrain her excesses of confidence. 'My
friends are more concerned about how much we have to compromise
with the outside world. And also how much we have to compromise
within the Ivory Tower of Yale . . . do I write a paper the way they
want so that I sound just like them or do I write a paper the way I
want and get a horrible grade? My teachers think I have too much
confidence. They call me The Mouth.'

To get the best out of university life most students pursue as
many non-academic interests as they have time for and Jodie was
no exception. She joined in with various campus activities, handing

out programmes at a Bonnie Raitt concert and serving as a witness in a Yale Law School Barristers' Union trial.

Soon it felt as if she had been living like this for ever and Jodie began questioning her old life. She was passionate about Yale and wanted to carry on with her academic life indefinitely. She simply couldn't imagine going back to the world of filming where she spent so much time holed up in a Winnebago waiting for her call to the set. She gradually stopped returning calls from agents and producers and found herself wanting to shake free of all that.

It was only natural, however, that she graduated towards the Calhoun College theatre set and she actually auditioned for a role in the Marsha Norman play *Getting Out*, about a former prostitute who serves eight years for murdering a cab driver. She played the woman – Arlie – when she was a young girl.

It was her first experience of the stage and although she was nervous of doing live theatre after the fragmented world of filmmaking, she loved the challenge of learning a new discipline. 'I get to scream a lot which I've never done before. The hardest thing about my part is that a lot of the time I'm not speaking directly to anyone. I have to remember when to speak and what age my character is at the time.'

For the part, her hair was unwashed, her clothes baggy and her language tough. For much of the play she sat alone in the corner in darkness poring over a Bible. It was an emotional portrayal of the adjustments a woman has to make in prison and in a hostile world after her release. As the play starts she has just gone to prison for shooting a cab driver.

Used to the subtleties of filming, Jodie had a few problems in early rehearsals according to the play's producer Andrew Paulson, who explained: 'She had a couple of problems at first intrinsic to her work in film. She didn't project and she understated. But shortly after rehearsals began, these problems vanished.'

Paulson's crticism did not endear him to Jodie and may well have been a case of a young man trying to make himself look important at her expense by taking the credit for the improvement in her performance.

Jodie had a little trouble with her skin at this time and it erupted in pimples because of the greasepaint. But she found the whole experience so exhilarating that she honestly couldn't have cared less about her spots.

The director of the play was Tina Landau, daughter of film producer Ely Landau, who took her student cast to visit Greenhaven prison in upstate New York where they read scenes from the play to a group of prisoners, mostly in jail for rape or murder.

Tina Landau made a point of not picking Jodie out for comment when interviewed about the play, for which the teenage star was grateful. Jodie was thrilled to be part of it all. 'I love Yale totally. It's definitely what I wanted to do. I can go any place I want with my friends.' When reporters crowded around her she would insist they talked about the play and not her.

The play was halfway through its run when President Reagan was shot and Jodie's world exploded. She was 'skipping hand in hand across campus with my best friend. Someone yelled: "Hey, did you hear? Reagan got shot."' She didn't know it but her nightmare was just about to begin.

Nobody would have blamed Jodie for quitting as a result but she insisted on finishing the two-week engagement. A small army of FBI and Secret Service agents along with New Haven police kept a watchful eye on her, checking everyone entering the playhouse.

There were no problems selling tickets. Jodie's unwelcome notoriety ensured a packed house every night and ticket touts were getting $50 for a $5 seat. Jodie considered backing out but the play would have had to be cancelled without her. The role of Arlie wasn't the main role but it was a big part and she decided that she needed to prove to the world that John Hinckley was not going to ruin her life.

During the final days of the play's run, Jodie had to deal with another incident that came close to shattering her fragile confidence once again. She had asked for cameras to be confiscated from members of the audience as she was particularly aware of the sound of a camera motor-drive.

She focused her attention on the spot where she believed the culprit to be sitting and directed her character's most cutting lines to one of three people sitting in a row until her eyes picked out a bearded man in the middle who was not the photographer but who held her attention by staring at her in an unnerving and emotionless way.

He did not flinch once as she hurled her character's lines at him and although it worried her, nothing happened. The next night he was there again in the same seat and so was the clicking of the camera although it was coming from a different position.

It was during the interval of the third performance of the weekend that a note was found on a lobby notice board stating: 'By the time the show is over Jodie Foster will be dead.' As it happened it turned out to be a nasty joke by a couple of students who were angry at being frisked when they went into the auditorium.

Strangely, Jodie felt only relief. After all, she had survived and no harm had been done. She was more concerned about the photographer and questioned him angrily. She was particularly furious when she found out that he had been let in by the producer.

A few days after the show ended, a death threat was delivered under the door of her room. Cool as a cucumber, Jodie passed it over to the authorities as she had been told to by the police.

Whatever emotions were bubbling under the surface, it was important to her at that time to carry on as normal in public. The years she had set aside to be a student were too important to her to be thrown away because of this. And whatever the reactions of others, especially the press, her brain was telling her that the assassination attempt was not her fault.

She would probably have been fine had it not been for the revelation that the man in the audience had intended to kill her. It was a grim few weeks during which she reached the depths of depression before making an almost superhuman effort to pull herself together and decide she was going to see it through and not let it beat her.

She felt she owed it to herself after the effort she had made to attain the life of a Yalie. She reckoned that she had done a pretty good job of fitting in at Yale. People had accepted her as one of them. Her appearance, her clothes, her whole attitude were so far away from the Hollywood star that she deserved to be allowed to fade away into the crowd. She had managed it before Hinckley arrived to shatter her peace and she would do it again.

Nevertheless it was impossible to be utterly anonymous. There were plenty who were curious apart from the regular stream of press photographers who hung around the campus. There were several tales of besotted young men. One just wanted to kiss her dormitory door.

She was friendly without being loud, modest without trying to hide her achievements in the film world. People liked her and with a small circle of friends she was gradually able to be young and silly again, to laugh and joke and behave like students always have done.

She was a familiar sight in Cross Campus Library, where undergraduates studied, her fair hair falling about her shoulders, a small frown of concentration on her face. After a few months of the starchy college food her cheeks began to fill out and she began to look less like the skinny Hollywood actress and more like a chubby freshman.

Jodie and her friends would work till late then order in pizzas at midnight. During her first year she put on about 20 pounds in weight. It was partly comfort eating, something to do to take her mind off the Hinckley incident and the way in which she had been thrust into a role she had no wish to play. For the first time in her young life she felt out of control; if not quite a victim, then an unwilling participant in somebody else's drama.

Publicly she adopted a flip, wise-cracking veneer. 'You just have to go on. I don't think about it. Who would want to hurt me? I'm such a nice guy,' was typical of her response to questions from other students.

It was inevitable that her work suffered as a result of the disruption caused by the assassination attempt and Hinckley's subsequent trial. There were missed classes and disappointing grades. Photographs of herself in newspapers appalled her. When she saw them she realized that she was fooling nobody with her 'tough kid' act.

At the time, however, few people would have guessed at the turmoil she was suffering. For months she was shadowed by security guards. The university authorities particularly were afraid they might be liable if there was an attack on their most famous student. Paparazzi stalked her from dormitory to lecture hall. Student stringers for New York gossip columns watched her every move.

Then there were the cartoons and jokes in the newspapers and on television – like 'Why did Israel bomb Lebanon? . . . To impress Jodie.' Everywhere she turned she seemed to hear her name being spoken, or some reference to Hinckley. She resented it bitterly.

She felt considerable anger during the months that followed the shooting. Crowds upset her. She was suspicious of every passing stranger. As more sick letters arrived she felt she had become the focus of every nutcase in the country. She read them all and struggled to understand why such people should want to hurt her. She said: 'I was being followed all over the place so I had to go around in people's trunks, take freight elevators. It was a rough time for me. I suppose I went a little crazy.'

She stuck to a small circle of friends and especially to a young New Yorker, Marco Pasanella, with whom she had a close relationship. The pair were inseparable throughout that term and could be seen daily studying in the library, doing crosswords or eating in the campus coffee bars. For her safety she was moved into what was affectionately known as a 'psycho-single', a single room which was in a more secure block where there was a warden who kept an eye on everyone.

After her summer examinations were over, Jodie threw herself with relief into a new project, a film called *O'Hara's Wife*. There had never been any intention of abandoning filming completely. The long summer vacation was set aside for movie-making and she was even prepared to skip a term if the right part came along.

O'Hara's Wife, with Ed Asner, was a fantasy about a hard-working lawyer whose late wife's ghost comes back to goad him into giving up the rat race and taking a trip around the world. Jodie played Asner's wise-cracking daughter. It was a role she carried on throughout the year when interviewer after interviewer tried to pierce her armour and find out how she had been affected by the events of March 1981.

The following year she decided to take a term off to make a television film called *Svengali* with Peter O'Toole in New York. It was an update of the old tale and Jodie played a rock singer who thought she couldn't sing without the help of her voice coach, with whom she falls in love, played by O'Toole.

Coincidentally one of her old school-friends was O'Toole's daughter Kate and Jodie struck up an easy friendship with the lanky Irish actor. She began to laugh again and O'Toole teased her gently, nicknaming her 'midget' and 'snot-nose'.

He felt genuinely sorry for the dignified little girl-woman who had been through so much and described her as 'a gutsy little bird'.

Then forty-nine to her nineteen years, he became a temporary father figure to her while on screen they played lovers. 'It is all so unfair that this tremendously nice, talented and hard-working girl should have become the target for every nutter in the land,' he said about her. He was amazed that she was so un-neurotic.

She in turn appreciated his kindness and called him 'gazelle legs' affectionately. 'Working with Peter has been wonderful. I don't remember when I laughed so much,' she told a reporter. It made her fall in love with acting again and helped to heal the wounds that didn't show.

O'Toole's illustrious track record and friendships with literary figures impressed her immensely. She said: 'He's wonderful and amazing. He's known everybody. Dylan Thomas was his room-mate. And he knew Samuel Beckett. That's like saying he knew Aeschylus.'

What O'Toole thought about *Svengali* is not recorded. It was hardly Oscar-winning stuff but it paid a few bills for him and took Jodie's mind off her troubles for a while.

A bodyguard was hired to make sure no other cranks got to her as she filmed on the New York streets but the only trouble was when a photographer tracked her down and Jodie dealt with him herself, dashing after him and demanding his film.

It was an upsetting incident and it happened when Jodie was feeling physically at a low peak. She had a sore throat and was nursing a broken collar bone. All in all she was feeling rather sorry for herself one evening as she was making her way back to her hotel. Suddenly a flash bulb went off in her face. The next thing she knew she was running down the street after the photographer, slipped, and came down on her injured shoulder. As she lay there sobbing all she remembers was the photographer's triumphant shout: 'I got her! I got her!'

She felt bitter and angry but managed to get herself back to her hotel room where she wept herself to sleep. By morning, however, she had regained her self-control and made light of the incident.

Director Anthony Harvey was impressed. 'She's a very adult woman. Naturally inside I think she was churning up but she never showed it. When she was pursued by a photographer she took after him. She caught up with him, got the camera and took the film out. She skinned her knees but I thought "good for her". He'd been waiting all day. It seemed unfair somebody would do that.'

When *Svengali* was finished Jodie returned to college to continue her studies resolutely determined to carry on as normal and in public at any rate, refusing to dwell on Hinckley as if the very mention of his name might shake her resolve.

In private, however, she was still hurt by the experience and it took her a long time to get over it.

She would be drawn reluctantly into commenting on the connection between *Taxi Driver* and Hinckley. It was the inevitable question in interviews and she dreaded it. She was defensive about the film. 'Films do as much good as they do anything. It's like a piece of sculpture. Anything you do can be interpreted in any way that the human mind feels necessary. I mean, I could kick a can and something could happen. Or, if I wrote on the walls, it could have an adverse effect on somebody. You don't censor art because of anything like that.

'And another thing is, exactly how much involvement film-making had to do with any of this has been purely a figment of the media's imagination. Political figures are actors too, they're characters and they have as much influence over what people do emotionally.'

If Jodie ever needed a complete change of scene she needed it now. The summer vacation of 1983 was spent in Montreal making *The Hotel New Hampshire*, based on John Irving's best-selling novel about an eccentric American family. For a few months Jodie allowed herself to soak in the quirky, off-beat atmosphere engendered by director Tony Richardson.

The other actors included Rob Lowe, Nastassia Kinski, Paul McCrane and Beau Bridges. Jodie played the central role of Franny Berry, the smart-alec middle sister between a gay brother and a straight one with whom she has an affair. She also has a lesbian relationship with Kinski's character, who spends the entire film wearing a bear suit. In one scene she kisses Kinski. It was typical of the strong victim roles that have attracted Jodie all her working life, and once again she found herself the target of moralists who found the film strong meat.

But making the film was a fun time for Jodie. The cast stayed in a small Montreal hotel, eating their meals in the classrooms of the disused convent school the film unit had taken over. Rob, Nastassia, Paul and Jodie were roughly the same age and eased the long hours between takes by playing practical jokes on each other. Jodie also took the opportunity to do a profile of Nastassia for the American magazine *Interview*.

Kinski is one of her closest friends in the business but it didn't stop Jodie dissecting her in an analytical, although affectionate, way.

> The funniest part about Nastassia is, she's supposed to be the prettiest girl in the world but she thinks she's incredibly ugly, she considers herself grotesque. That's why she can't trust anyone who says they love her. It's like 'God, if you love me, you must be a real jerk.'
>
> She's always got food on her face, her clothes always have big stains on them, she'll wear Nikes with suede pants – she's out of it, a real space cadet, but that's what I love about her.

The experience of making the film was like stepping from one university campus into another. The young actors lived and behaved like students. One day Paul McCrane arrived on set just as Foster and Kinski were rehearsing their love scene. The two girls suddenly looked up in horror as they spotted red-haired McCrane standing under a particularly powerful arc-lamp and shrieked at him to get out of its beam before it turned his hair green. They told him urgently that the best remedy was vinegar. McCrane rushed off and found a pair of purple silk panties which he soaked in vinegar and wore on his head until his co-stars' hysterical laughter told him it had all been a joke. The following morning McCrane turned up for filming with his hair sprayed bright green and wearing a dead-pan expression. He carried off his joke so well that someone seriously suggested running for the vinegar.

Director Tony Richardson positively encouraged this sort of fooling around. It helped establish the quirkiness of the film, and the laughter eased any embarrassment the two girls felt during their brief screen kiss. Kinski, who took the role in the first place because of her year-old friendship with Foster, said of the kiss: 'It didn't feel foreign at all.'

After years of being a grown-up little girl on set, always professional, always on time and word perfect, Jodie enjoyed what she described as a regression into immaturity. She said:

> This professionalism that you learn growing up in movies – always prompt, being quiet, I don't think I've lost that, but I've also got to be laughing all the time, I've got to have people around telling jokes constantly. There comes a point when you just want to veg out and watch *Charlie's Angels* or *Love Boat*. I'm incredibly immature. Though I suppose there's a maturity in consciously pursued immaturity.

Neither she nor Kinski was entirely happy about the script, so they simply set about putting it right. Foster's intelligence, academic background and years of experience making films allow her that sort of luxury, which producers might not tolerate in other actors. There was a distinct sense of intellectual arrogance about her in those days which she was not bothered about hiding. She told one interviewer; 'I've rewritten parts of every film I've ever done. When you're on the set, there's a certain sense of what works and what doesn't that some guy just out of UCLA will never have.' She got away with it because she was generally right. Today, however, she would be more tactful about doing it.

While Jodie had no qualms about portraying incest and lesbianism on screen she was still unusually coy about nudity, and rowed with director Tony Richardson over her refusal either to take her clothes off or to do a rape scene. 'I'm never nude on screen. Never have been. Tony Richardson and I had this big fight. He said, "If you're going to be an actor . . ." I said, "Fine, I'm not an actor and it's going to look stupid because I'm not comfortable with it." 'As usual Foster got her own way. The clothes stayed on. And although a rape scene was the focal point of a film which was to win her an Oscar a few years later, she simply wasn't ready for it at this stage in her life. 'I didn't need to play that scene because of the one that followed it, but you could argue that it was my laziness . . . I get what I want and it's a very safe way of not dealing with something. Tony Richardson could have forced me to do it but didn't.'

There were endless mealtime discussions on other subjects, with Jodie enthusing about the Afro-American writers she was studying, often assuming that everyone else knew as much as she did about them. When she gets started Jodie can certainly talk. For somebody who insists that she is a 'very private person' she gives little nuggets away unwittingly in every interview she does.

She would spend hours analysing her character in the film and drawing parallels with her own life.

It doesn't bother me that a lot of my unconscious motivations have to do with the character. *The Hotel New Hampshire* is after all a transitional piece, it's about people growing up and what makes a blank page a full page – the events that shape your life.

My case and Franny's are perhaps a little more extreme than in 'real' life, but basically it's the same thing . . . Franny's identity changes in terms of every character she gets involved with. Only toward the end does that character become defined in terms of herself. It's a classic interpretation of what it is to go through adolescence and become a post-adolescent.

I love the movie because it shows how much you have to go through to become a person. There are a certain number of events that shape you and that are an important part of your personality and that should not be shooed away as horrible, suffering moments. They're really a part of you.

And that's one of the things that most adolescent films today don't contain. They're just about having sex for the first time. And I really don't think that's the be-all and end-all of adolescence.

One film buff noted that the movie contained a couple of typical Jodie Foster close-ups in which she is smiling at first and then her face becomes pensive. Jodie agreed that it's a trademark.

It's unconscious but I know I do it all the time. I think it emphasizes that anything you do or feel may have a double significance. You feel good about something but then you don't. Also we keep a lot to ourselves that we don't tell other people – the hidden side. I love the written word but that kind of silent gesture is what tells most about working in film.

Her friendship with Rob Lowe developed as the weeks went by, but once again it was platonic. There was no love affair. Jodie felt comfortable with friendly, good-looking types like Lowe but didn't want a sexual relationship with them.

He's like my little brother. We had a very strong kind of fraternal relationship. It's funny because people's image of Rob is very different from my image. My image of him is as a kid who wears glasses and we'd hang around my hotel room and he knows *Wizard of Oz* by heart and we'd lie on the floor most of the time and laugh hysterically and play Monopoly or whatever.

And I don't know him as a sex-symbol guy with an earring and a leather jacket. I mean, he wasn't like that. But I do recognize the fact that he is incredibly handsome and terribly charming and funny. He's one of the funniest people I've ever met in my life. But that's how I feel about my brother. My brother's handsome and he's charming and he's funny.

Lowe was intrigued by the girl for whom somebody shot the President, but was hesitant about bringing up the subject of Hinckley with his new friend. Later he said:

The first thing you think about when you hear about Jodie Foster is that horrible business. I wasn't going to bring it up. The first night we met for dinner she brought it up. It was almost as if she had to talk about it. She said she'd gone through the mill, that things couldn't have been much worse. If someone can come out of something like that the better for it, she has. She's wiser and more wary.

She's serious but not totally so and that's what's great about her. She's very bright – she reads everything in the world – but she can also have fun lying in bed in her pyjamas watching *The Jetsons* [a television cartoon].

Rob would tease her and they'd laugh together about their personal idiosyncrasies such as Jodie's meticulous attention to detail. 'Rob asked me why it is that I get so much pleasure out of knowing that I'm always on my mark. You give me a mark and I'll be on it. I think it's the stability,' she laughed.

Stability is something she has always strived for. She likes order in her life, and the discipline of filming was one she embraced and felt comfortable with. It was as if the roles she chose were helping her grow up. She has often said the clues to her life are in her work. She finds it easier to talk about herself in relation to the work she is doing at the time.

Part of the reason why *The Hotel New Hampshire* was so special to her was the strong family-type ties she made on the set. There was genuine sadness when it was all over

When *New Hampshire* came along, I said to myself, 'I know why I do this, to be here and be with seventy-five people and feel this way.' With Rob and Nastassia I really felt we were family. We were dangerous – all those things you hate about kids – catty, obnoxious, loud, saying mean things about people. I believe we achieved a certain reality you don't get in mythic films. The part where I end up sleeping with my brother and then say, 'That's it, goodbye, here's to the rest of our lives!' always touches me.

When we finished the picture, we were all teary-eyed and drunk and we knew we would never be like this again. That's the way intoxication is. You lose something – what you were – and you take in something. It was like falling in love for the first time. It wasn't a hierarchical thing and it wasn't just the actors – it was also the boom man, the prop guy . . . I could have howled at the moon stark naked and walked on that set like a crazy woman and known that I could trust them.

Still on her leave of absence from Yale, Jodie took herself off to do another film, this time in Paris. In *The Blood of Others*, based on Simone de Beauvoir's *Le Sang des Autres*, a Second World War drama directed by Claude Chabrol, Jodie played a dress designer's assistant living in Paris, involved in an impossible love affair with a resistance fighter. Jodie became the first American actress since Jane Fonda to dub her own part in French.

Ironically, at that time Jodie had not the slightest interest in couture clothes. Her student wardrobe consisted of baggy jeans, oversized shirts and tee-shirts, with plimsolls on her feet and a rucksack for a handbag. Other people, usually her mother, would buy her 'smart' clothes for her. She managed one foray into the chic Paris stores but was easily diverted. 'I just can't go shopping. Yesterday, I decided I would go shopping once while I was in Paris. I came back with two "superballs", you know, the kind you played with against a wall and they bounce back.'

Chabrol watched her with interest both as an actress and as a person struggling with emerging adulthood yet hanging on to childhood. He saw her stride on to the set, dazzling in a black chiffon dress and rakish black hat, with hair set in Veronica Lake waves, deliver her lines and then retreat to her dressing room in inexplicable tears, only to emerge later, jaunty and cheeky, bouncing her superballs. He said: 'She's strong, she's intelligent. She protects herself . . . but also she wants to stay the child.'

While she was in Paris finishing off the film she received the news that the jury had found John Hinckley 'not guilty by reason of insanity'. Shocked by the verdict, she cancelled her flight for New York and headed for the Black Forest to stay with friends. She needed a rest away from telephones and newspapers where she could take in the news without prying eyes.

It was a stressful time for her just when she was beginning to pull herself together, and, like many students, she experimented with alcohol as a release from pressure. Other stimulants were readily available on campus and among film crews. It wouldn't have been surprising if Jodie had resorted to them at this time. Just before Christmas 1983, she was returning to Los Angeles from Europe when she was stopped and searched by customs officials at Logan Airport in Boston where she was changing planes. They found a small amount of cocaine in her luggage.

Under US law, possession of a gram or less of cocaine does not necessarily require formal charges. Jodie admitted that the white powder was indeed cocaine and officials decided not to prosecute, simply fining her $100 and putting her on a year's probation. She was later orderd to pay court costs of $500. Jodie's lawyer, John Gilmore of the Boston firm of Hill and Barlow, told the judge that someone had given her the cocaine at a party.

There was no huge public outcry or shock waves, either at the news that Jodie had been found in possession of a drug or at the mildness of the fine. Even court officials appeared to take pity on her, and her forty-five-minute appearance in East Boston District Court the following January was kept secret because of death threats against her. Mark Newman, an assistant district attorney who was then head of the Suffolk County drug unit, said his office let Foster slip into Boston unnoticed not only because of the death threats but because the media had distorted this 'very insignificant case'.

We don't want to give the public the impression that all the drug work being carried on by this office is focused on her. She was treated basically like any individual in the same factual situation. She had less than one-tenth of a gram and was charged with being in possession. She had no record at all. That would be the standard recommendation.

She has an outstanding record as a citizen and academically. Everyone who knows her speaks highly of her and she has no prior involvement with drugs.

The general feeling from the public was that it was unsurprising after what she had been through. It could have been worse, and it seemed to shake her out of her depression.

She began to work on her weight and general fitness, and took up kick boxing to get rid of her aggression and tone up her body; she also thought it might come in useful if she was to pursue the independent life she sought. Jodie was coming to terms with the fact that somewhere out there might be another 'crazy' planning to harm her or finish the job that Hinckley had started, and she might as well be prepared.

Her grades began to improve and she started to enjoy her studies once again, particularly the philosophy of literature and the work of the black American novelist Toni Morrison, on whom she wrote her senior thesis. Jodie was fascinated by politics and feminism, and Morrison's novel *Tar Baby* inspired her. 'When I read her book I said, "Yeah, that's good writing." I don't think there's a bigger compliment than "You really made me lose my breath",' she said.

At one time she seriously considered a career in writing herself. She enjoyed crafting a sentence, exploring the language. Debate stimulated her, and the world of politics attracted her briefly. But in the end her love of acting and her ambition to direct pulled her back to her roots. She said: 'I don't want to be plagued by my own expectations for the next few years. I'm still young and I don't want to be saying, "Next year I'll run for the Senate" or "Next year I'll write a book." One advantage is that if I make a hit movie I don't have to learn to cope with being famous overnight.'

The years at Yale took on a pattern – eight months of studying and four of film-making. It was almost a double life, and she loved both. She seldom brought up the subject of Hollywood unless she was asked about it – she had never been used to pouring out her feelings anyway. But another young actress, Jennifer Beals, the star of *Flashdance*, was also a student at Yale and the pair became friendly. Few of her other friends were interested in the world of acting, and she found she could talk to Jennifer about the other side of her life.

In her final year Jodie and another close friend, Jon Hutman, moved into a two-bedroomed apartment which they delighted in decorating with photographs of Nancy Reagan and an inflatable paddling pool hanging over the couch. It was kitsch – full of plastic ornaments and dime-store rubbish – and Jodie loved it.

> My apartment is so great. It's in such bad taste. For the first time in my life I could say, 'Fine, everything is going to cost me 25 cents, I don't care.' So we – me and my room-mate – keep the price tags on the furniture. It's only pink and green. Everything's tacky, everything. We have diner furniture, train sets. We have a blue plastic robot, a blue plastic swimming pool on the wall. People hate it. I love it. We have Christmas lights all year. On the door it says, 'Welcome to the New Mall.'

Jon was and still is a dear friend who helped her shed her ghosts and settle down again to being the carefree student she expected to be when she went to Yale. An architecture student, he was, like Rob Lowe had been, purely a friend and not a boyfriend. He said at the time: 'We do live together, but we're just room-mates.' The pair shared the same interest in the theatre and liked the same people. They would cook meals for each other or 'pig out' on hamburgers. It was the nearest thing Jodie ever got to rebellion. She was away from the dominating influence of her mother and wallowed in self-indulgence – of both the intellectual and the culinary kinds.

Her weight was gradually coming under control – she had put on a lot in the two years after the Hinckley episode. One classmate remembers an incident when Brandy arrived for a visit and sought her daughter out in the library where she was studying.

In a particularly insensitive way Brandy shouted: 'Hey, Jodie, you've got too fat. You've got to lose it.'

Jodie turned pink with anger. The classmate remembers: 'Everyone turned around and I really felt sorry for her. She was really angry.'

She was, however, determined to do her own thing at college. She was very aware that the years were rattling by and this was an opportunity never to be repeated. She said: 'There's something about losing your childhood once you leave college and it scares me to death. I don't want to have my tax returns and my *New York Times* on the table for breakfast. I just do not want to do it at all.'

So while she revelled in the fun she was having, she was also a dedicated student and would retreat to the library or her minimalist Japanese-style bedroom where she would pore over her books for hours. She was neat and methodical in her approach, making good use of her time, a habit formed as a child when she had to fit in her school work during breaks in filming. She was in addition constantly on the look-out for unusual roles which would test her as an actress and ideas which would stretch her as an academic.

Yale was a positive experience and one that she still values. But four years was enough. At the end of her time there she had no wish to go on to graduate school. She said:

> I learned how to read in the larger sense of being analytical, of not looking at surfaces and thinking, 'That's what things are.' And I did well because I'd work from nine through five. The other students were always sitting around saying, 'Oh, man, I just can't get my stuff finished.' Mine was always ready two weeks before it was due.
>
> I had some scholarships to pursue a PhD programme. But, when it came down to it, I realized that I was good at literary criticism, but it wasn't a life or death thing. I couldn't see myself

fighting for that stipend or working all night on that Nietzschean commentary. What's right for me, as an overly intellectual person, is to have a career that makes me passionate and upset and happy because emotions are not a real big part of my personality.

Her Yale years taught her to see the relevance of her studies to the rest of her life. Literature in particular took on a peculiar significance to the craft of acting.

> Something suddenly hit me and I realized that literature wasn't an escape from movie-making but that I could incorporate and analyse literature in making movies. And that made movies interesting. Acting wasn't interesting for me when I was growing up. I thought it wasn't stimulating enough but I wasn't putting enough into it. I wasn't looking at acting in a way that didn't have to do with the profession.
>
> But if there is anything that is absolutely relevant to directing movies it's going to a class in Greek tragedy or looking into Lacan or Freud or looking into the French Nouvelle Vague. Whatever it was that I did there it was more relevant to the way I look at movies now or the way I'd look at movies as a director than sitting around talking with my chums about who got to audition for *Top Gun*.

During her four years (1980–4) in New Haven she did just enough film work to keep her career ticking over. 'I did six films while I was there. I never had a vacation during college, ever. When I had two weeks off I was either somewhere looping [dubbing film dialogue] or going on a publicity tour. Or else I was finishing a picture while I was doing exams on the set.'

At that time in her life, however, it was of prime importance to prove to everyone and especially herself that she was no airhead actress. She would never have been satisfied with a third-class degree. She had to 'go for broke'. It was part of being a winner. 'There were a lot of things I had to prove to myself. I was not going to get out of there with Cs. And I was not going to go, "I'll take home economics" or "I'll just take three courses a term." No way was I going to do it half-assed.' She graduated with honours in 1985.

Above all, the break from Hollywood made her realize that she actually did want to be an actress. Before that she hadn't really thought about it. Acting was just what she did for a living. Yale allowed her the time and space to grow up and make decisions about how she was going to live the rest of her life. 'I always thought all actresses were stupid and believed if I went to college I wouldn't turn out that way. But I realized what I really wanted was to be an actress and there was nothing stupid about it at all. It's like going to another country – you learn about chopsticks and all that, but what you really learn about is yourself.'

EIGHT

The Accused –
The First Oscar

Jodie Foster is not one of the silver screen's great beauties but she can be beautiful when she wants to be, and as she has matured she seems more inclined to pose for glamorous magazine spreads. Small-boned and petite, her face is strong rather than conventionally pretty with deep blue eyes and a pointed chin framed by fair rather than blonde hair.

However, people seldom realize that, like Scarlett O'Hara in *Gone with the Wind*, she's not conventionally pretty. On screen something magical happens. The camera loves her and she projects beauty.

In her usual analytical way she understood all this at an early age. She knows she cannot compete in the drop-dead gorgeous stakes with the likes of Geena Davis or Michelle Pfeiffer, and she doesn't try. 'When I was growing up in LA – a city of classic beauties – my edge was my education and my verbal acuity,' she said.

That is certainly true, but as the years have passed Jodie has learned how to be absolutely stunning for the camera. Mel Gibson found the transformation fascinating when he was working on *Maverick* with her. One minute he would be talking to the girl-next-door, then off she'd go to make-up and come back a bombshell.

In 1987, two years out of college and twenty-five years old, she was just beginning to understand her strengths. But after the trauma of John Hinckley and her subsequent battle against her weight the swan had not yet emerged from the ugly duckling.

Daily visits to the gym and energetic work-outs were having the desired effect, and once she finally shed the weight she vowed never to pile it on again.

Her obsession with secrecy and her desire to go unnoticed in private makes her favour the scruffy look – she calls it 'schlumpfy'. She said: 'There are times when you don't want to be the centre of attention. That's 95 per cent of the time for me.'

Playwright John Patrick Shanley, who wrote the screenplay for *Five Corners*, said: 'I don't think she understands how complicated she really is. She has a lot of technique which she doesn't like to talk about. When she walks on to a set, it's obvious she's done a lot of preparation. She can do something extraordinarily natural and repeat it five times. It moves you.'

Five Corners is set in the Bronx in the early sixties and tells the story of a rough neighbourhood during a thirty-six-hour period. Jodie played Linda, an ordinary working girl who has a job in a pet shop and wears plain cotton dresses and a Sandra Dee hairdo.

She decided to do the film, another of those which sank without trace but which earned her personally good reviews, because she was impressed with the originality of the script. Shanley, the son of a meat-packer whose father's ambition for him was to get a job in the Sanitation Department, grew up in the working-class Bronx where gang fights were an everyday occurrence. His thirst for education – after a spell in the Marines he went to New York University and graduated with honours – mirrored Jodie's own, and she worked for a fraction of her fee in order to be part of what she saw as a worthwhile project.

As with so many of her parts, her character in *Five Corners* becomes the victim of a love-crazed man's obsession, but her claim that the similarity to her real-life experience did not cross her mind when she read the script for the first time seems improbable given her intelligence.

I play a together girl in the Bronx, who has a boyfriend but is terrorized by this big dummy who's been in jail and is completely obsessed with her. He decides to take her away. I get knocked over the head and carried around unconscious in John Turturro's arms for about 40 per cent of the movie. Very King Kong. But it's also about a neighbourhood that no longer exists, about that lost innocence.

It has a very weird and artsy script by John Patrick Shanley and Tony Bill was the right director for it, because he could strip it down to its simplest level and make it accessible.

It never occurred to me until I started shooting it that there could be any comparisons in my own real life. Even my Mom didn't think of it. When I read the script I laughed at some of the scenes. But when they were played so well, so menacingly, by actor John Turturro, they seemed scarier.

She was irritated by the assocation and the fact that it kept cropping up in interviews. She was desperate to distance herself from the incident, believing that it somehow trivialized her and detracted from her ability as an actress.

It really annoys me especially since I had no responsibility for it. I want people to go see my films and be interested in me as an actress.

I took this film because it's the best screenplay I've read in a long time. It has a very strong narrative – it's realistic as well as mythic and is about an era that interests me. I'm not of the school where I look for juicy parts, and I don't do films because psychologically I could learn something about myself or because the character is something I always wanted to play. A lot of people do, but that doesn't interest me as much as doing a good book. I look for good films.

During the film's shooting she lived in a tiny cluttered apartment in Manhattan filled with plants, books and studenty bric-à-brac. She prefers to have her own bolt-hole rather than staying in a big hotel where people stare at her.

Her existing interest in the technical aspects of film-making developed, and she would spend hours with the sound men and the camera technicians learning about their jobs.

It's not very glamorous but it's the part I like best. Long hours and wretched food. Like going to school. There's a real sense of collective work about it, collective art.

The challenge of film acting is to succeed despite the odds – no matter what your blueprint is, you're never going to wind up with it. You're doing a love scene, for instance, and there are seventy-five people around.

I'm more interested in making good movies than in getting to cry. You're talking longevity as well. I want work for the next twenty years.

Already her mind was turning towards directing, which she was beginning to see as the real challenge of film-making. She was constantly on the look-out for the right script to cut her director's teeth on. 'The thing about directing is to know what you want and to be able to get it from people twice your age. And I can't afford to do a half-assed job,' she said, using one of her favourite expressions. Her language can at times be fruity.

Although she missed the intellectual stimulation of Yale and the discipline of writing papers, she had decided to turn her formidable intellect towards learning about life on the other side of the camera. In the meantime she suffered the indignities of the acting profession with good grace and humour – curlers in her hair, for example, for her part in *Five Corners*. 'This Sandra Dee look is no joke. You gotta suffer for it,' she laughed.

Making movies was her bread and butter, and at twenty-five she had made as many films. 'That sounds as if it were some grand plan. It is grand but there was no plan. I've been doing this for so many years that I'm more comfortable in front of a camera than anywhere else. In later years she was to admit that she had made several bad choices, but they had seemed a good idea at the time. Her compulsion to keep working regularly, the 'Protestant work ethic' that drove her, made her convince herself that a project had merit when nowadays she would turn it down.

Stealing Home was, perhaps, one of these, starring the handsome Mark Harmon as a failed baseball player who is made responsible for the ashes of a friend, played by Jodie, who has committed suicide. Jodie only appears in flashbacks. The critics dismissed it as a 'baseball movie', of which there were several during that summer of 1988. Jodie typically defended it. 'It's not a baseball movie. It's a sentimental education about what people are made of. It's about the series of consequences, people and events that touch you during your life and make up what you are. What's that to do with baseball?' What attracted her to the film, she claimed, was the 'hero-type relationship' she has with Harmon's character. 'She is what he would like to grow up to be. I've always wanted to be a hero for someone – and that's someone I've always wanted in my life too,' she said.

Perhaps because she felt honour-bound to do publicity she would rather not have done, she appeared prickly in interviews. She didn't mind putting herself up for the inevitable dissection by the press if the film was dear to her heart, but *Stealing Home* evidently was not.

I'm tired of people trying to psychoanalyse me. It seems to be the new trend in interviews these days, to try to figure out Jodie Foster. I don't know why they do that. They don't do that to Morgan Fairchild.

I suppose it's because they've watched me grow up in public. They've watched my personality grow, my smile change and my gestures develop, so they think they're an expert on me. Well, they don't realize that there's nothing to figure out.

My goal is longevity in this business and the plan is to accept roles that are different. If I did a comedy, I next did a drama. If I did an artsy film, I followed it with a down-to-earth film.

I don't want to be in a $35 million film that doesn't say anything. As a matter of fact I don't do big films at all. I guess that's why I'm still working. I don't put all those nooses around my neck and I don't make those billion-dollar errors.

And the result is that I'm very happy with my life right now. I like where it's been and I'm sure I'll like where it's going. I know there's some place else to go, but I'm not sure where it is.

She argues convincingly but the truth is, as with any other actress, that you have to go with what's around at the time. If there isn't an Oscar-winning part in the pipeline, and you want to keep on working, you have to accept the best of what there is.

The attraction of working with 'bad boy' Dennis Hopper, whose wayward youth gave him the reputation of being both wild and brilliant, found her in the Mexican desert after *Stealing Home*. 'He's very sexy and very, very attractive. It's his naughty boy past that makes him so attractive,' said Jodie, who played a woman who witnesses a mob killing and falls in love with the hit man sent to kill her.

The film, called *Backtrack*, was never released in the cinema but came out on video in 1994. Jodie revelled in the beauty of the rugged pink Mexican desert, which was so different from anywhere she had worked before. She spent her free time exploring. 'I hate to admit it, but I'm one of those outdoorsy types. It was a real thrill cruising around in the desert, hiking those gorges and all that stuff.'

In many ways Jodie was underselling herself with many of these films. Perhaps if she had displayed a little more actressy temperament and been less professional she might have raised her profile. But that was never her way. Instead, she carried on going for films she felt had some merit and waited for the big one.

It came in the form of an adaptation of a real event in which a twenty-two-year-old woman called Cheryl Araujo was raped in Big Dan's bar in New Bedford, Massachusetts. At around 9 p.m. on 6 March 1983 Cheryl, wearing tight blue jeans and a figure-hugging pink sweater, only called in to the waterfront bar for a packet of cigarettes. On the way out she tripped over a man's leg jutting across her path. Suddenly she found herself pushed on to the floor and her jeans torn off as more than twenty pairs of hands groped her. She was dragged at knifepoint to the back of the bar where she was pinned down on a pool table and several men took turns to rape her. She lost count after six. Other men cheered and yelled encouragement to the rapists before Cheryl managed to escape around midnight and ran out of the bar, where she was picked up by a lorry driver who took her to hospital.

Her ordeal scandalized America and hundreds of angry women held a silent, candlelit protest vigil outside the New Bedford bar where it had occurred. Eventually six men, the sons of Portuguese immigrants, were arrested and tried, four for rape and two for being accessories. They claimed that Cheryl acted provocatively and 'asked for it' by dancing by the jukebox. Four of the men were found guilty and jailed for terms ranging from six to twelve years, but two were cleared of holding Cheryl down during the rapes and were set free.

Cheryl's life ended sadly three years later. Unable to escape from the stigma attached to the rape, she slammed her car into a lamppost at 90 m.p.h., killing herself and seriously injuring her two young children. She never saw the film which was based on her tragic life, but among feminists it caused as big a furore as the real event and it appealed to Jodie Foster for the same reason.

Her capacity for serious homework means that she gets her hands on almost every script going in Hollywood. In 1986 when she read *The Accused*, originally called *Reckless Endangerment*, she knew the part of Sarah Tobias was one she wanted. 'I did everything I could to get it,' she said.

Director Jonathan Kaplan had worked with Jodie on another project, which had come to nothing. Although he was aware that others felt Jodie carried too much baggage with her in the form of the Hinckley affair, he was impressed with her honesty and professionalism and was convinced she could do the part. Producers Sherry Lansing and Stanley Jaffe weren't so sure. Jaffe favoured Kelly McGillis for the part of Sarah, but Kelly had her own very personal reasons for refusing.

Kaplan telephoned Jodie to set up a meeting with Jaffe. 'He wants to see if I'm still fat,' was Jodie's immediate response. A star with her track record should not have needed to test for a role, but she has never been one to stand on her dignity and since she badly wanted the part she agreed to a screen test. Its impact was so strong that, after watching it, Lansing prophetically remarked: 'The envelope, please' – a reference to the Oscar presentations.

Set in Seattle but filmed in Vancouver, *The Accused* was the second major highlight of her career, the first being *Taxi Driver*. It was the film that saved her as far as the studios were concerned, and put her back in the front line as an actress. 'It was another landmark for me,' she said. 'It's a dream part, a gift.'

Sherry Lansing, who co-produced with Jaffe – the same team which produced *Fatal Attraction* – said that her aim was to make a film about the guilt of the bystander. 'We also wanted to change people's perceptions of rape, to show that the victim always has the right to say no.'

Sarah Tobias is neither the usual heroine nor an out-and-out victim. She is a tough-talking, pot-smoking, whisky-drinking good-time girl, a waitress who lives in a trailer with a loser for a boyfriend. When she is raped in a bar after dancing sexily by the jukebox, just like Cheryl Araujo was supposed to have done, nobody is very surprised. Even the female prosecutor, played by Kelly McGillis, is prepared to do a plea-bargaining deal because she doesn't have much faith in Sarah as a witness. Sarah, however, is furious and tells lawyer Katheryn so in no uncertain terms, prompting her to reopen the case by laying charges of criminal solicitation against the men who cheered on the rapists. The explicit and violent three-minute rape scene comes as a flashback towards the end of the film, and drew criticism for exploiting sex and violence under the guise of condemning them.

Jodie passionately defends the film and the right of a woman like Sarah to the same justice that a more educated person would receive.

It may seem surprising but in a strange way this was an uplifting film to make. Every day we came home from work knowing we were doing something important. Important on a practical level, to encourage people to report the many rapes that go unreported in this country. Important to women in opening up a topic which is still largely taboo. And important to men and women both, to encourage them to discuss, to create a conversation.

I think I grew up on this film. It was the first time I ever admitted to myself that I was an actress as opposed to acting being something I was doing until I grew up. I think I've always disassociated myself from that part of me. Acting was a job I did – but I wasn't an actress.

Her words echo the feelings she had making *Taxi Driver*. She was aware that this was another landmark in her development as an actress.

In many ways I feel this is the most important film I've ever done. It wasn't always fun – it was often very difficult to do – but you don't make movies just because they're fun. There are sometimes deeper reasons and certainly there were for *The Accused*. I wanted Sarah to be able to prove herself, to be a good witness, to find her own voice, to prove to society that she could rise above their low expectations of her. If I did that, I'll be happy.

Just four years before, Jodie had refused to do a rape scene in *The Hotel New Hampshire* which she thought was gratuitous, but this time there was no escape. The rape was the core of the film. It was an emotionally draining experience; the actual rape scene was particularly difficult for everybody, especially Jodie.

That scene was the hardest thing for any of us to do but it was what the whole picture was about and we would have been wrong not to tackle it. It was hard on everybody – on the men even more than the women. We did it first and it bonded the company together. We would finish shooting and then hold on to each other and cry.

It is as difficult and uncomfortable to watch as it must have been to film, and Jodie cried so hard that she broke blood vessels in her eyes. She put so much of herself into it that she became moody and difficult with her friends, although she has always denied that she is a Method actress who lives the part.

Years later, she admitted to having had incredible panic attacks about doing the rape scene. At one point she really believed she couldn't do it, she wasn't up to it.

> I just said to everyone, 'I can't do this. And I'm so sorry that I ruined your movie.' I thought it was the end of my career.
>
> I couldn't talk about it for a long time. It was so hard to admit that it was a difficult movie for me. I laughed, I joked, I made friends with the guys who played the rapists. But here's how bad it got – after I got the part I never bothered to read the script again. I got to the set and bullshitted about the story. I was acting so cool and now when I think about it, I was petrified.
>
> I was so incredibly vulnerable. Screaming at my friends even. It was challenging and very miserable and very intense. I know this sounds like a 'very California' thing to say, but it's true. Half the time people were laughing hysterically and throwing their arms around each other. Or they were crying, having nervous breakdowns and fits. And I'm only talking about the crew!

Canadian actor Bernie Coulson, the key witness at the rape, recalled the day they started shooting the scene. 'We all thought, "Oh great, Jodie Foster is going to be naked." But that wears off pretty fast. Then after four days of seeing these guys with flesh-coloured G-strings pumping her, at one point I just turned away and threw up.'

It took five days to film, and by the end of that time crew members were coming up to director Jonathan Kaplan and complaining that they were losing sleep and their marriages were suffering. They wanted to move on to another scene.

Said Kaplan: 'I insisted that we shoot the rape first. I thought if she had already filmed the rape, that experience would flood forward when we shot the courtroom stuff. But her own life experiences – the whole John Hinckley business – had trained her not to get emotional in the courtroom and she held back at first. In her screen test, the only thing missing was deep rage within.'

Brandy Foster wept when she saw takes of her daughter on the court-house set and was worried about the effect the experience was having on her. She stayed with her on set for several weeks, taking her for long walks every night and trying to keep her calm.

Jodie admits that if she can possibly make things easier for herself she will, as far as doing a scene is concerned. Not for this one, however. This time she gave it everything she'd got. In fact she insists she simply blanked out the horror of the rape. 'When I got off the table each day I didn't remember anything. Usually I remember the flies, the microphone, every little thing. Here, all I could do was grab my make-up woman and hold on to her and cry.' It was also typical of her that she was more concerned about those around her and their reactions. She felt the need to play mother hen to them all, and went around comforting them. One actor in particular cried every time he looked at her, and the cameramen had to shoot around him.

Even allowing for the tendency of Hollywood folk to over-dramatize and the obvious desire to beef up the drama of the shoot itself to encourage people to go and see the film, it is still a searing scene and Foster is magnificent. She was high on adrenalin for days after the rape scene was shot. 'For a whole week I couldn't eat or sleep. I was delirious. I felt that way during the entire film.'

For Kelly McGillis it was almost unbearable because she had been brutally raped herself. But she bravely talked about it because she too was convinced of the importance of the film for women. In 1982, when she was a student in Los Angeles, two men broke into her flat and found her alone in a bathrobe. They raped her at knifepoint. The police, who were called by a neighbour, arrived twenty-five minutes later.

McGillis spoke frankly about her ordeal in an interview in the American magazine *Maclean's*. 'I was raped by two men in my apartment – strangers. For a long time I wanted to forget that it happened. Unfortunately I remember every minute of it. It changes your life for ever. I will always be afraid to be alone. I will never know what it means to be safe.'

Somehow her pain and the pain Jodie had suffered over John

Hinckley created a deep bond between them, a friendship which has occasionally been misinterpreted as something closer. What is certainly true is that they developed an intense relationship and spent a great deal of time together both on and off the set.

As with the friendships she developed with Nastassia Kinski and Rob Lowe on the set of *The Hotel New Hampsire*, Jodie would spend hours talking to Kelly and Jonathan Kaplan on *The Accused*.

> It never occurred to us that we were being boring. Normally when I am making a film I am able to switch off and watch TV when I get home. But doing *The Accused* was so stimulating I just couldn't get it out of my mind.
>
> Jonathan, Kelly and I really connect in a basic, homebody way. I could have a spat with Jonathan like I would with my brother and the next day I'd apologize and it would all be forgotten.
>
> It's like family with Kelly too. Pretty soon after I met her I felt she was my sister.
>
> As a performer she has really taught me things. Some had to do with her training but most came from the way she thinks and feels. I say things off the top of my head, but when Kelly says something it's usually dead-on. She really knows what she's talking about. She's completely astute, never haphazard like I tend to be. She's also deeply emotional. I'm not saying I'm not emotional, but I've had to live in a different world than Kelly has. It hasn't hardened me but it's given me sun block. Kelly doesn't repress anything. She's very real and she doesn't lie. She can't. She doesn't know how to.

The intensity of their friendship was not dissimilar to that of the friendship she has with Nastassia Kinski, whose big-eyed, high-cheekboned beauty bears a resemblance to Kelly's. 'In the past, except on *New Hampshire*, I was never pals with other actors. You work for two months and the last thing you want to do when you're not working is talk about acting.'

Jodie is almost obsessive about her close friendships. She needs to know about every aspect of the loved one's nature. 'I'm compulsive, passionate and perfectionist – about virtually everything. I'm that way about my friendships. I want to know everything – absolute details, entire lives – because that's when I feel passionately bonded.' The relationship of the two women on film was crucial to the movie. Said Foster: 'It's a psychological drama. It's not specifically about a relationship. It's really how characters evolve by bumping into each other. It's about how your life is changed by circumstances.'

As always with Jodie, she needed to believe she was doing something important, for a purpose. She hated to do anything trivial, and it was only with *Maverick* that she decided she can allow herself to have some fun on screen rather than always working on films that have 'messages'.

But for the present she was making a film with a hugely important message. 'Specifically what's wonderful about this movie is you're forced to come to love and respect someone who has all the attributes society thinks are unimportant – intuition, emotion, sensitivity, vulnerability. And she is frustrated by her lack of language. In fact that's what's been oppressing her for twenty years.' Sarah Tobias was real, and Jodie was totally committed to the part.

McGillis, who is now married to a millionaire yacht broker in his forties, Fred Tillman, and has two children, said,

> My own rape was very much why I did this film, very much the reason I wanted to be involved. At the same time I feel very strongly about not using my work as therapy. I don't look on it as cathartic and it wasn't.
>
> I had my choice of the two parts and I chose the lawyer because she was a greater challenge to me as an actress. She goes against everything I believe I am. Certainly I have an emotional reaction to sexual assault and rape crimes and Katheryn doesn't. What I hoped was that the film would help give other rape victims a voice, that it would open up the whole subject for discussion.

Both women were adamant that they wanted to expose the double-thinking surrounding rape. If a woman is provocative she 'gets what she deserves'. If a man cannot restrain himself, he's often excused. Jodie denies that it is a 'man-hating' film, but emphasizes that the relationship between the two women is of prime importance.

> Somebody said, 'Is this a feminist film?' Well, yes, I don't know any films worth their salt that aren't feminist, because a movie that contains a woman as a human being is a feminist film. But I don't think it's man-hating at all.
>
> Men see happiness for women as something external. 'If I give you a diamond bracelet, you will be happy. If I marry you, you won't be yelling at me.' Men think that 'I can't make her happy.' Women understand that happiness is internal and that you can't be in a relationship if you don't start liking yourself a lot.

Nor does she think the violence of the rape scene was gratuitous. It's what happened, therefore it was justified. 'Violence is part of life and the film demonstrates that it doesn't take a bayonet or shotgun or the army to commit violence. It just takes people. That's the frightening thing. The cruelty is human cruelty.'

Once they had all recovered from the emotional mangle of filming the rape scene, Jodie's attention wandered as usual to the technicalities of film-making. Said Jonathan Kaplan: 'Most of the actors were to be Canadian. Before we went up, Jodie took me aside and told me what to look for in casting Canadian actors. Later, she was the first actress I've ever worked with who'd come up and tell me I was wrong about something that had nothing to do with her.'

Kaplan's words were affectionate: he likes and admires Jodie. But it wasn't surprising that along the way she had acquired nicknames like Miss Authoritiva and BLT, for Bossy Little Thing. She simply couldn't help herself. If she felt something was wrong, it was not in her nature to stand back and say nothing. Because she was so friendly with the technicians and the make-up artists she knew what they were thinking, and for that reason people like the director listened to her when she made one of her frequent suggestions.

Kaplan, while listening patiently to Jodie, was not in the least overawed by her and would often tell her quite brutally that she wasn't doing it right. Said Jodie: 'The first day I walked on the set, he came to me and said, "Stop it. What are you doing with your hands? Do you have any idea how stupid that looks?" Nobody had ever said that kind of thing to me, but you get used to it after a while. He's the best actor's director I've worked with in years.'

The director was not above putting her in her place, but he was big enough to take her advice when it was good and in many ways they moulded a crew together. 'I play Florence Nightingale a lot,' she said. 'I always end up being recruited into getting the prop person back on the movie when they quit.'

When Jodie herself needed a little tender loving care, her mother was on hand as usual.

> She doesn't usually come to the set but I've come to realize I need someone familial for the first couple of weeks, because I not only get lonely but disorientated. I have a real bravado about my ability to go to a foreign place and be normal, but I get crazy. I can adapt easily to bad things. I can adapt to never going to sleep or to whomever I'm around. If they never wash their face then I won't wash mine. So I have to watch out about that. And my mother is the best person to travel with because she does whatever she wants. When I'm in a bad mood, she can say, 'Shut up, you're in a bad mood!' and I can say that too, which I can't with my friends – they'll hate me for ever.
>
> I can implicitly trust my mother. She's not going to take my money and go to Paraguay, which happens to a lot of people. When my mom says, 'I think you should do this,' it's not because it's a good idea for me to do it. She's a friend, more and more so. She's always been my friend.

For some reason Jodie felt unsure of the performance which was to win her an Oscar. When shooting finished she was convinced that her performance was hopeless and she actually considered postgraduate work again. 'I was gonna go to Cornell University and be a grad student in literature and no one would ever hear from me again. I'd be found out as a fraud. The film was just very provocative for me personally,' she said.

However, it was soon clear that *The Accused* was arousing passionate interest and discussion in the media on both sides of the Atlantic, and Jodie realized that it was a hit. Police and courtroom attitudes to raped women were examined, and the dilemma of a woman going to court and being treated on the one hand as a victim and on the other as a slut was questioned vociferously by feminists. The movie addressed the issue of whether or not a woman has the right to dress and act in a sexually provocative manner without being accused of 'asking for it'.

Jodie defended herself against accusations that she always portrayed women as victims.

> Someone said to me, 'You call yourself a feminist and yet you play victims in movies.' But can you tell me that being a victim is not part of womanhood? If I portray a victim, does that mean I'm not Wonder Woman? Well, I'm not trying to be. There are a lot of ugly things in our history, as in black history – and the truth has to be told. You can't censor art through 'political correctness'.

Prominent women were canvassed for their views, among them the mother of one victim, Suzy Lamplugh, who went missing in 1986. Mrs Diana Lamplugh, who has campaigned to make women safer in the workplace ever since her daughter's disappearance, felt the film had two messages. 'The courage of the girl in her determination to bring her aggressors to court delighted me. One of the things women can do in the midst of this epidemic of sexual violence is to insist that the world takes rape more seriously.'

She had reservations, however, and feels that women must take responsibility for themselves and try not to put themselves into needless danger.

> I do think the film has another message and that is that although no woman deserves to be raped she should not get into a situation where she is not able to say 'no' quickly enough. There is no

doubt that in the film the victim's ability to protect herself is diminished by the fact that she had drunk alcohol and smoked marijuana. She did not realize that she was going too far. Youngsters need to be taught.

The Accused changed many aspects of Jodie's life. After it she found she no longer had a taste for lightweight 'ensemble' films. Although the film was not universally praised, one review after another predicted an Oscar for Jodie and she found she could afford to be picky as her worth per film soared. She could wait for the next big movie, the big director. At the same time it restricted her personal choices. The pile of rejected scripts in her living room grew higher by the day. 'I know what I don't want to do any more and that seems to be making my choices smaller.' Once those choices were made, however, Jodie was pretty sure that a project would be developed. It made her even more conscious of her self-imposed responsibility to do valuable work and not to be phoney. It also made people remember her for something else than being the actress for whom some nutcase tried to kill the President. The shadow of Hinckley would never leave her, but it was receding.

She heard the news that she had been nominated for an Academy Award when she was on a plane heading for Europe to promote *The Accused*. 'A man from Alitalia came right out on the tarmac and the people on the plane clapped for me. It was nice,' she said. Even after the Oscar was firmly hers she could hardly bring herself to believe she had won it. 'Sometimes I'm driving down the freeway and I'll just start laughing. It just hits me. It's scary, too. What if I fail next? What will people say?'

When it was all over she did what she always does between films. She went home. Not for her an exotic holiday in some fashionable watering-hole. She would head straight back to the San Fernando Valley, where she has always felt safest. She said:

> When a film is over I don't know what comes over me. For three
> weeks I have to dance. I go to all the clubs and spend three hours
> on the dance floor with my friend just having convulsions. Then
> I go back to the Valley where people don't want to hurt you.

When I'm away from there I always feel like everyone wants to hurt me.

I tend to surround myself with people who are not emotionally indulgent. Actors create drama in their lives so they can feel. I'm not like that. I don't like to stand out. It makes me worry. The best gift my mom ever gave me was to get me to stop worrying so much because I kill myself worrying.

If she needs a retreat she will occasionally hide away in a Japanese-style hotel – the New Otani, for example, in Los Angeles – where she sleeps on a futon, eats sitting cross-legged on the floor and cleanses her body with relaxing massages and aromatherapy baths.

What really relaxes her is staying at home and cooking for friends, watching soaps on television and working out at the gym. She likes routine. When she doesn't have to be on set early in the morning she will set herself a rigid exercise routine to keep her body in shape. Every day at the same time she will drive to the gym and do a session lasting about two hours. It's almost obsessive. 'An actress has a duty to be versatile with her body. Anyway, it's better than being compulsive about alcohol and drugs, isn't it?'

On top of the visits to the gym there would be tennis and karate classes. Kick boxing was another phase. It is all part of her professional attitude. She feels a compulsion to give directors their money's worth, and that means keeping herself in peak condition of fitness. 'I'm not a competitive sports person, but I go crazy when I'm not doing something. I'm not in pursuit of the body beautiful. Like learning, it's more of a discipline – gruelling, difficult, completely absorbing. It's the one time of day when I don't think about taxes or films.'

Kelly McGillis remembers a visit to the gym with Jodie. 'I had to do this nude scene in The Accused so I thought I'd lift weights to get big chest muscles. Jodie kept me at it for three hours and she never let up. I became closer to her than any other actress. She's very smart, a total professional. I like that.'

Being professional is just a way of life to Jodie, who said:

As a child you learn that to be professional is your number one priority. The art comes second. You learn that to give your best performance you have to be a good technician. Out there you've got to be on top form. There are no excuses. If your dog dies on the set, if your child is wheezing with leukaemia, it doesn't matter. If you have problems, it's something to apologize for, to be embarrassed about, not to revel in.

At this stage in her life, as now, work came first. No effort was too great if it concerned a film she was making. Off screen it was different. 'Sometimes I'm a jerk. Everybody is. Sometimes I can screw up. I get irritable. I can get really mean in traffic. I yell at people. But I couldn't live with myself if I was a jerk on set. I never storm off sets. If I did I'd have a heart attack.'

In an interview in *Vanity Fair* a year later she did her usual self-analysis about her compulsion to look after everybody and above all to control everything around her – something that was to become an all-consuming part of her character as she grew older.

I wish I weren't such a sponge. I wish I didn't always think it's my job to deal with all of it, to be the cruise director and social repairer. That's why I loved working on *The Accused*. Jonathan would direct the other people and I'd go along with my little sweeper, tidying up so he could do his job. But now I'm realizing that you can't be a woman and be twenty-five years old and be totally together – and that I have such a complex about always being in control.

It was another watershed, a time when she took stock of her life and reassessed where she was heading. She called it her 'mid-youth crisis':

It's only recently that I've come to feel it. Because I suddenly got to one of my goals. You finish college, you spend six months in bed, you do four pictures and then you have to take a new step. I've never been anywhere without a big predictable step ahead of me. Now I'm not sure what the next step is. And the failure element is much bigger.

As far as the trappings of success were concerned, she still could not bring herself to acquire them. Perhaps the comparative poverty of her early life, full of style but short on luxury, made her unwilling and uncertain about spending her hard-earned cash. She still lived in a small rented apartment and drove a ten-year-old Volkswagen.

But she was beginning to be more assertive and less acquiescent about things that annoyed her in her personal life.

> My whole life, people have flaked out on me. They don't show up, they're late, and I always figure, OK, they're busy, I completely understand. If I wait for you a half-hour in a restaurant, it's OK, but now I really think, No way! I hopped all over town, I made all this food. I bought all this wine and you didn't fucking show up! Why am I supposed to make you feel better when you flake out on me?

She found it frustrating that people always took her so seriously. They would ask her questions that required a thoughtful and often intellectual response, so she came across as quite a serious person when another side of her just wanted to laugh and have fun.

> I guess people don't see how immature I am. I'm really immature in a lot of ways, not in ways that I'm ashamed about. I think people think I'm incredibly self-sufficient and I can take anything. On shoots it's actually a detriment to me. Because it's like, 'Oh, a tall building that's on fire – put Jodie on top.' They get me to do things nobody else will do.

Surprisingly, just when she was beginning to stretch herself as an actress, she talked about knowing her limitations. 'Some actors don't know their limitations but I do. Why reach for great heights that you can only fall from? And you don't have to be smart to be strong. Dumb blondes can be strong.'

After the emotional high of making *The Accused*, Jodie resigned herself to the inevitable wait before the next major film. Her compulsion to keep working led her to do a strange surrealistic film directed by Mary Lambert in Spain; but *Siesta*, in which she managed a passable English accent as a dizzy Sloane Ranger type, bombed.

At the same time Jodie began seriously to pursue her other ambition – to direct. It was the habit of a lifetime to read scripts, and when she heard of a good storyline being turned into a script she would track down the writer and beg for first sight of it. It gave her an edge over other actresses, and she was prepared to fight for a good part when it came along. She found the story of *Little Man Tate* in a pile of rejects and tucked it away in the back of her mind until the right opportunity came along.

NINE

The Silence of the Lambs – The Second Oscar

On a chilly night in January 1990 the security man on the door of the Los Angeles morgue was surprised to see the diminutive figure of Jodie Foster waiting to be admitted. She was welcomed by veteran coroner Claude Boucher, who gave her a detailed and unsettling tour of the place two weeks before shooting began on *The Silence of the Lambs*.

Jodie was to play FBI trainee Clarice Starling, who hunts a serial killer who skins his victims. For her, imagination alone was not enough: Jodie needed to see for herself what a dead body looked like. 'You can't make a movie like *The Silence of the Lambs* which ultimately deals with the pain and horror of death and not have death in front of your eyes,' she said.

For four hours she toured the building, stopping to look at a male burns victim lying on a slab and wondering aloud why a person wore a particular pair of shoes or shirt the day they died. She talked to staff about picking up bodies and bringing them to the morgue, asking them about their feelings and questioning them about the circumstances in which they found the corpses. She wanted to know details like how long fingernails grow after a person is dead, how a body shrivels and what happens to the skin. She saw the body of a young man with a gunshot wound in his head, and fell silent when she was shown the room where the dead babies were kept.

For weeks she immersed herself in the real-life and often gruesome world of police work, spending two weeks at the police

training academy at Quantico, Virginia, with Special Agent Mary
Ann Kraus, on whom she partly based Clarice. Mary Ann, thirty-
six, described as one of the FBI's top agents, showed her photographs of murder victims at the notorious Black Museum, and Jodie
listened to the screams of two girls tortured to death in the back of
a van by a pair of multiple rapist-killers. Mary Ann said:

> They taped the girls pleading for their lives and screaming. It was
> the most harrowing thing imaginable but Jodie heard it as part of
> her research.
>
> Jodie was deeply affected by everything she saw but she didn't
> flinch from any of it. We thought it was important to give her
> the reality and she was very quick to learn, very professional. She
> even went up to Pennsylvania where a female murder victim had
> been found and attended the autopsy. That's a harrowing thing to
> have to do, especially for the first time. If she was going to play
> an FBI agent she had to understand what the role would be at an
> autopsy and how she would have to act.

Mary Ann, who has seen more horrifying sights than she cares to
remember, was impressed by the way Jodie handled herself. 'My
main aim was to show her around the academy and make her
familiar with the way we do things. But it was also important she
realized the sad, sick truth of what goes on. She wasn't forced by
anybody to see the things she saw but she chose to and I admire
her guts for that.'

When agent Kraus saw the results of Jodie's research on screen
she found them chillingly realistic. In particular Sir Anthony
Hopkins' performance as Hannibal Lecter disturbed her. 'I have
spoken to men like that in prisons and institutions and they are just
as Hopkins portrayed Lecter. He made my skin crawl. I have
learned to live with the reality but the fiction on the screen
disturbed me. There are people like that out there.'

Jodie was made aware of the particular outlook of the FBI
agents, people who 'have a bigger agenda than personal gain'.
Although she has reservations about many of the institutions they

preserve, she nevertheless wanted to see them portrayed accurately and in an honourable way.

Jodie's obsession with the seedy and terrifying world of serial killers began when she read the best-selling Thomas Harris novel *The Silence of the Lambs* and knew instantly that she must have the part of Clarice, just as she recognized Sarah Tobias in *The Accused* as an ideal part for her. When she heard that *Silence* had been given the go-ahead she tracked down screenwriter Ted Tally and lobbied him for the part. Later she went to Orion Pictures and Jonathan Demme, the director, who had Michelle Pfeiffer in mind. Jodie phoned him and begged him to consider her as his second choice, just in case it didn't work out with Michelle. Said Demme:

> Michelle read it and it became apparent that she was unable to come to terms with the overpowering darkness of the piece. I had recently seen *When Harry Met Sally* and was crazy about Meg Ryan.
>
> Jodie's resumé was all over the chart, but I loved that whatever she'd done, it was never terribly far from the edge. And I liked what she felt was important about *The Silence of the Lambs*. She believed it. This, for her, was the opposite of some bullshit movie story. Her identification was with a character who felt deeply for victims.

It was the very darkness that disturbed Michelle Pfeiffer which intrigued Jodie, and at a meeting with Demme she simply talked him into giving her the part. Jodie has absolutely no feelings of inhibition based on false pride when it comes to going for a role she wants. 'You fight for the ones you have serious personal connections with,' she said simply. 'I had to fight tooth and nail for *The Accused* and I don't find it humiliating. It's like "So what?" I got the performance and the Oscar, so – what?

'I was in New York and had a meeting with Jonathan and you know through the grapevine who he's leaning toward so I basically said, "I want to be your second choice. These are the reasons I want to make the movie. They are very personal reasons. Not just that it's a good part. So just give me a call." '

Said Demme: 'She helped me understand the character better. Frankly, she connected me with some of the scenes I became preoccupied with in the movie. And she made me realize that we'd be very fortunate indeed to get her to play the part.'

Jodie was fascinated by the notion of Clarice, a specialist in behavioural science, as a hero who used her intelligence, rather than the brawn she lacked, to trap the killer. She was also concerned that the FBI agents she had made friends with at Quantico should not be misrepresented. 'I'd really gotten to know some of them and like them a lot. And I said to Jonathan, "There are two things I'm afraid of with this picture. One is that it's gonna somehow glorify murder. And the second is that it's gonna make fun of these crew-cut government people."' Demme was able to reassure her.

Getting behind the mind of a monster was almost a personal crusade, hence her commitment to the gory autopsy scene. 'There's a body on the table, murdered with grotesque mutilations. So there's a certain basic horror, of course. And compassion for the victim. But the more my character gets into the work, she experiences a kind of exhilaration. She's excited. She wants to get inside the skull of the man who did this,' said Jodie. 'Once Clarice sees the first corpse, she's so bonded to this quest and her identity is so immersed in it that nothing else is possible. She can't think of anything else. So it's almost something that she has to free herself of.'

It was Jodie's first real venture into the world of big box office. The subject matter was another departure, scarcely politically correct and involving two serial killers, one who skins his victims and makes their skin into dresses and the other, Lecter, who bites off faces and disembowels his victims. Who can forget Hopkins' chilling description to Clarice of how he eats their livers with 'fava beans and a fine Chianti'?

The FBI uses her as its pawn to manipulate Lecter into helping them catch the other killer, known as Buffalo Bill. At the core of the film is the duel of two powerful and complex minds. Director Jonathan Demme said: 'It's the first character I can think of where Jodie didn't have to hide the intelligence she possesses as a person.

I think she's always had to mask that one way or another. I wish you could have seen how effortlessly she would suddenly be Clarice Starling.'

As usual Jodie plunged with vigour into the actual business of putting a film together, never seeming to mind the unglamorous slog of getting up before dawn in sub-zero January temperatures to go to work in a vast steel shed in Pittsburgh once used as a turbine factory.

The life is what Jodie has always known. It's as if she almost expects to be uncomfortable when she's working, as if her work isn't worthy if it's too cosy.

> To me, eight months out of my life every year was spent getting up at the crack of dawn, eating shitty food and drinking shitty coffee and making things work – getting dirty and tired and sunburned, just doing it. So I guess I grew up with that ethic and I was never as ambitious about the other stuff as everybody else was. My aspirations were always, 'When can I get back to work and hang out with a new group of people, learn something new, go some place new.'

Jodie, who had her hair dyed a rich dark brown for her role, is proud of the way she presented Clarice.

> I built that character – it's one of the most true and progressive portrayals of a female hero ever. I feel proud that we didn't say 'Here's a hero because we pumped her full of steroids so she would look like a guy.' Or 'Here's a hero because she is really sweet and nice and that's why we like her.' The truth is she's a hero because she has tragic flaws. She faces things about herself that are ugly and while facing them she solves the crime. This is hero mythology and that has never been applied to a female character in film, ever.
>
> A small woman can't employ the same methods as a muscle-bag. It's not about machine-guns, it's about the capacity of intelligence to combat the enemy.

It was a change for Jodie to play a hero rather than a victim. Once again she felt this self-imposed responsibility towards other women in her choice of role.

> She's such a complex character – somebody who's all about what she's not admitting. She's a rural person who's desperately trying to become an urban person or someone who has a fear of the mediocre, fear of being average.
>
> It's a very complicated pattern and a problem that isn't addressed very often. It's the responsibility of the studios in some ways to start developing female heroes and educating the audiences about them.

The on-screen chemistry between Hopkins and Foster was electrifying. 'He was really scary. When I first saw him he was behind bars. The chemistry came out of the words, intimacy through eye contact. When I finally saw the film finished I bolted a bit but I don't see it as a gory film. It's quite sensitive and deals with the problem of serial murders effectively without going into grand gore.'

Jodie found working with Hopkins an enriching experience. Her first meeting with him was 'unnerving'. Hopkins, as Hannibal Lecter, began to improvise, making fun of Jodie's accent as Clarice.

> He was in the middle of something and then he started imitating my accent. The first time he did it, I wanted to cry or smack him. I was so upset. You're in a scene, so you sort of feel those things, but as an actor, having someone imitate your accent – it just killed me. It was the perfect thing for Lecter to do, because Clarice has been hiding her rural accent, trying to speak better, escape her origins in a certain way. And here's a guy who nails her.

She may have been shocked by the clever cruelty initially, but the verbal and mental interchanges fascinated Jodie as much as they did Clarice. The intensity of the scenes where Lecter questions Starling about her past pleased her.

> It is an absolutely intimate experience. And I think it's the closest to psychological therapy. It's about revealing something that's

never been analogized. What I love about that scene is that it's about the small things. It's not about 'And then I was five!' It's about things that shape you and form you analogically in ways you never thought they did before.

It's also a symbolic and literal trade-off. It's this idea of combatting your villains or coming to terms with your guiding force as a hero. And coming to terms with things that are petty, things that are small, that fit into your powerlessness in order to become a powerful hero.

She could have been talking about herself. She has a compulsion to identify with roles in some way. As Sarah Tobias in *The Accused* it was the character's strength and what she saw as nobility which enabled her to triumph over what seemed like overwhelming odds stacked against her. In *Silence*, it was Clarice's mental dexterity and her single-minded pursuit of evil that appealed to her.

Hopkins found Jodie friendly and professional. 'She is very pleasing to be with, very easy. She is very cool, calm and collected and very accessible. We didn't become great friends or go off to dinner every night. At the end of the day she would go her way and I would go mine but I liked her enormously.

'She invited me to a football game once. There was a big game in Pittsburgh but I'm not a great sports fan so I said "No, I would be bored." She didn't mind. She just said OK.'

He admired her skill as a film actress, especially in close-ups when, for example, Lecter would let out one of his sudden hisses. 'The close-up on her face was excellent. She works with such economy. She doesn't do a thing and yet you can see all the thoughts going through her eyes, like, "Oh my God, this man is an animal, a beast." And I think that's the great skill of an actress like Jodie – it just shows on her face, she doesn't have to act it.

'She works like me – she keeps it really simple. She doesn't need two hours in the corner first. I think that's the real mark of a mature actor. She draws upon her great concentrations, that centre of stillness and calm, and then she just does it.

'She comes on set with only a cup of coffee and a sense of determination to do a good job.'

Jodie in turn admired and liked the Welsh actor – 'he's the nicest guy you'll ever meet. He's this funny, gentle, nice man. He's genuine' – who became protectively paternal towards her, especially during demonstrations from militant gays who protested at the portrayal of Buffalo Bill, the serial killer, as a homosexual pervert and demanded that Jodie should declare herself as a lesbian.

Compared to more recent 'politically correct' films like the 1994 winners *Philadelphia*, starring Tom Hanks, about a lawyer stricken with AIDS, and *Schindler's List*, about the Holocaust, *The Silence of the Lambs*, basically a horror movie, was an unusual choice for an Academy Award. But it swept the boards at the 1992 Oscars ceremony, winnning best actress for Jodie, best actor for Anthony Hopkins, best director for Jonathan Demme, best screenplay for Ted Tally and the best picture award. It also won a host of other awards including the Golden Globes, the New York Critics' Association awards and BAFTA, the British 'Oscars'. It was the cinema's biggest blockbuster since *Batman* and the smash hit of 1991, costing £20 million to make.

The second Oscar established Jodie in the big league among actresses, and she had done it without compromising her beliefs or allowing herself to be manipulated by the Hollywood star system which demands that its females be glamorous. Jodie has never been defiant, simply sure that her way is right for her. Her strength was and is her strength.

TEN

Little Man Tate –
The Director

In a stifling hot warehouse in Cincinnati Jodie Foster was smoking furiously. A small frown of concentration appeared between her eyebrows as she worked out how she could juggle the shooting order of the scenes to accommodate a nine-year-old boy who is only allowed to work a certain number of days a year. To look at her nobody would have believed she was happier than she had ever been in her career. She may have had problems, but they were solvable and they were her responsibility, her decision alone. For the first time in her life she was totally in charge. She was Jodie Foster, Director.

It was the culmination of a lifetime's work in film and she was still not yet thirty years of age. She had just finished *The Silence of the Lambs* and was finally able to embark on shooting the film she had been working on for two years – *Little Man Tate*. Jodie had found the script among a pile of rejects, which she tends to read out of curiosity, sometimes just to keep up with what's going on in Hollywood and sometimes just to see where a bad script goes wrong. She immediately got in touch with the producers, Orion Pictures, and expressed an interest in playing the role of the mother and directing the whole thing. She had recently established her own production company, called simply Egg Pictures, and had been looking for the right project.

'I try to read everything that's out there – every script that's called a go script, which means it's going into production. This was a project with another director on it. Then the director fell out. So when Dawn Steel at Columbia said to me, "Is there anything you want to do?" I said, "Yeah, I read this one thing," and she said, "Why do you want to do that? It's such a small movie." '

Foster has never minded 'small' movies as long as they mean something to her, and this one carried echoes of her own experience as a precocious child actress. 'At first they didn't take me seriously, but after I helped with rewriting the script they realized that I was capable of doing the job. They told me I could direct as long as I could find a distributor – and I did,' she said.

Jodie has known she wanted to direct ever since she was about thirteen and worked with Robert de Niro and Martin Scorsese on *Taxi Driver*. But it was only after she won her first Oscar that she felt ready to do it and that it was within her grasp. Still, she met with plenty of opposition from people who thought she should build on her success with more roles in front of the camera and capitalize on her Oscar financially. She knew people would be waiting to see if she would make a fool of herself, but she was prepared to take the risk. She wondered: 'Will people think I'm using my clout? Or will people say, "All of those actors – they think they can be directors. What the hell do they know?" Well, I've said that many times myself. I see it and I completely see the reasoning behind it. But I've always tried to improve myself. I'm sure the first five days of movie-making everybody's sitting there with loaded guns saying, "How will we skewer this actor-director?" '

But after twenty-five years as an actress in roles ranging from soft comedy to high drama she knew she needed to move on, even if she failed. It would be standing still just to be in another film. 'You have three options when you win an Oscar. You either go for a juicy performance piece and another nomination; you use it to make a big movie that makes millions of dollars and you get paid a lot of money; or you use it to get you into something that normally you wouldn't have access to. So I guess that's what I did. Winning the Oscar helped me get the kind of budget I needed for *Little Man Tate*.'

The story is about Fred Tate, a gifted seven-year-old whose mother, Dede, is an uneducated cocktail waitress and a single parent. Dr Jane Grierson, played by Dianne Wiest, is a neurotic upper-class psychologist who wants to take Fred off to college and give him the intellectual stimulation he won't get from his mother.

Telling the story of a child prodigy drew the inevitable comparisons with her own life. She insists, however, that she was never a genius. The film is not about her, although she drew on her own experiences, especially on her relationship with her mother. But it is as revealing about herself as anything she has ever done.

> There are autobiographical splashes in anything and everything I do. That's one reason I do not work that much. The movie is personal, which doesn't mean it is about me. Although the fact that I chose this particular script reveals something about me definitely.
>
> The idea of growing up and being in some way set apart from the conventional society fascinated me.
>
> His intelligence is not the most fascinating thing about this boy. The fact that he is someone who feels deeply is much more provocative. That there are two sides to him – the mind side and the heart side – and how they interact, how these two sides confront each other and dance with each other is fascinating. The traditional dilemma about balancing two identities – the masculine and the feminine, the outer and the inner, the thinking and the feeling. Rather significant to an actor who has to balance the public self and the private self.

Jodie reacted strongly to questions about the rights and wrongs of taking a child like the young actor Adam Hann-Byrd, aged nine, who played Fred, or indeed herself, putting him in front of a camera and taking away his normal life. 'Normal life! Who wants a normal life? I don't. Normal is a kind of dirty word to me. Forget normal. I think healthy is more important. Yes, I think he can have a healthy life. This was an experience, this was more information about the world. I think information is only good so long as your heart is protected,' she said, speaking passionately to one writer and obviously basing her reply on her own experience of life. In fact she was utterly protective and maternal towards Adam, patiently explaining every move to him and making sure that he felt comfortable about what he was doing.

When they first met, Adam was quiet and reserved. Jodie won his confidence by doing some karate with him. She didn't fuss over him, but tried to treat him as she would like to have been treated at that age. She found him after weeks of scouring schools looking for a child who was like Fred Tate rather than a boy actor who would have to act the part. The amount of effort Jodie put into finding exactly the sort of boy she had in her mind and then, once she had found him, working to get the best possible performance out of him is typical of the way she approached every detail of her film-making.

We just went to schools to look. The first set of schools that we went to were gifted schools. The kids could have been any colour. It didn't matter because you never meet his father. We looked at lots of schools and different ages, from five years old to ten years old. Some little boys did have the right quality, but they couldn't read and stuff. Then he just walked in. He was doing his first play. I think he had two lines in it – it was about the Dunkin' Donut man or something like that.

He had a braided, blond ponytail. He wouldn't talk about anything. No chitchat, nothing. He would only look at his piece of paper. So we said, 'All right, fine. Do you want to run by these lines?' So he put the script in front of his face and stared at it and absolutely said every single word the way it was written. A fire truck went by. Somebody dropped something. All this stuff happened. I forgot my lines. But he never looked up. And at the end, after he was finished. he closed the script. That was it. That's what he thought it was about.

And I said, 'No–no–no–no, wait a minute. Sit here for a minute.' I tried to talk to him. He wasn't really interested in talking. He was painfully shy. All one-word answers. But when he was waiting for my notes on his reading, he looked at me absolutely in the eye and waited for me to tell him something. He just wanted to do it right. It wasn't like he had to deliver this great performance. It was all about the process with him. He wanted to do exactly what the task was that was asked of him and then he wanted to go.

Then I started working with him. I went to his house and we played. I said, 'You do karate and I'll do karate.' I made him try to hit me and push me. And he, of course, started laughing. I smacked him in the head and told him to smack me in the head. It was just about trying to get him out of himself.

When we were ready to videotape, he came in and did the 'Death' poem by Rilke. Our mouths were open. He had totally gotten it. There was no problem accessing the lonely, sad, thoughtful side of him. It was only the externalizing that was hard for him, because he's a little boy and he gets shy.

The character that Adam plays is in some ways not the giftedness part but the other part of being sensitive and analytical at the same time. I've always been just like that. When I was a little kid, I was sensitive to what was happening, to who was left out and who wasn't. And distanced enough to analyse it and talk about it.

When we were testing for boys I realized that young actors have this thing they've got to get over. There's such pressure for young actors, such competition, they feel that if they're not brooding Al Pacinos they're not acting, when in fact they're denying this huge range of behaviour.

She tried to keep it simple for him, gently taking him aside and telling him to 'Just pretend really well and then think about what that pretending looks like.' She said: 'It's a horrible way to teach somebody to act but, in a weird way, I think that's basically what it boils down to. The one thing I never did was I was never dishonest about what I was trying to do. I would never say to him "Your teddy bear is dead!" to solicit a reaction.'

For a few weeks she became a surrogate parent to the boy and found she liked the idea. 'Playing Adam's mother and guiding him was perfect. I loved the idea of the mother and the director being the same person.' Her own memories of being directed as a child made her want to do it differently with Adam.

> I did feel a need to protect him because I have been terribly burned in my life. I have had every kind of working experience, from good ones to hellish ones. Directors who scream at you, directors who never even talk to you on the set.
>
> I'd just say, 'Stand there and move your face when I say this line.' When I was a kid people would direct me like 'Are you ready' *sotto voce*. It freaked me out. It made me very self-conscious. You know, just tell me what you want. More angry, less angry. When I'm treated preciously then I can't perform. I get self-conscious and I feel like I'm not part of the crew and they'll laugh at me. I feel like I can't be safe.
>
> I guess I prefer kids more than anyone else because they have a certain purity. If a kid says 'I can't do that', you can't bribe him with an Oscar or more money.

Although many of her directors might disagree that she had no previous experience of directing – having been on the receiving end of her forcefully delivered advice – it was Jodie's first chance to use nearly twenty-five years of cinematic experience on a project of her own. She said:

> I've been ready to direct for a long time. I have a lot of experience on totally different-sized movies. And a lot of experience also watching movies fail, watching first-time directors fail. Emotionally, however, I don't think I was ready until after *The Accused*. There are only so many times you can make movies that nobody likes. At some point you've got to get some applause.

Her college friend Jon Hutman, the production designer on *Tate*, said:

> Jodie knows so much about film. Not only the day-to-day minutiae of how movies are made, but also what she knows from having been taken by her mother since before she could speak to

see all manner of films. Brandy's idea of a good time is going to three French movies back to back. And that was a large part of what Jodie's childhood was like.

Her greatest strength as a director was that she knew what she wanted. That's clearly why she wanted to direct. She'd done it other people's way enough times.

Jodie's approach to directing was based on creating a good working atmosphere for the actors and crew, surrounding herself with people she trusted to work the way she wanted them to. She also understood the importance of knowing each person she worked with well and finding out what motivated them personally. That way they could catch her if she fell down a hole.

You must learn to lead, to be a benevolent king. You try to communicate your vision and monitor those who don't get it. I feel safe there. I can be vulnerable. The code is they'll catch you if you fall down. I have a camaraderie with these people. It's like going through a war together.

I absolutely take their ideas. I'm not a director of photography or a propmaster, so you hire people whose language it is to design, shoot or accessorize the film. It is their language and your job is to guide it.

I have a very maternal relationship with my directors. With Jonathan Kaplan I really felt like he was behind my eyes. It's a very intimate relationship. Anyway, I didn't realize it when I was young because I was so busy doubting every director. I worked with a lot of first-time directors and – well, it's something I'm very careful with now that I'm a first-time director. You get excellent performances out of people – you have a chance of getting excellent performances out of people – when you know more than they do about themselves. Otherwise they'll just play something they know that works.

With Jonathan Demme, he really needs to believe that people are good – really nice, gentle, they're behind him. With me I don't really care about that. Egos I can take – if somebody is kooky or a jerk or talks about themselves too much, I can handle that too. But I really need people that are ultra ultra confident and not afraid of confrontations, and that's an actor thing. That's what actors do together.

The notoriously aggressive Scott Rudin, who co-produced the film, was impressed with the way she handled herself: 'I've worked with a lot of first-time directors. She was by far the most sure-handed in what she wanted – and knowing when she had it. She has confidence beyond what most people have as an actor or a director. She has confidence in herself.'

That doesn't mean to say there were no rows. She wasn't above 'throwing a wobbly' at times, and Rudin said she was occasionally 'unbelievably stubborn'. There were some casting and scripting disagreements which ended up in mini-explosions. At one point there were rumours that Foster had banned Rudin from the set. She wanted to develop the parallels she saw with her own life as a child actress, and Rudin wanted to leave the screenplay as it was. To his credit Rudin backed off and returned to help Jodie fight to get the budget she needed for promotion and release when Orion found itself struggling against bankruptcy.

Despite the pressures, which led to a relapse into almost chain-smoking, Jodie thrived on being in control. She said:

I love the stress of directing. I really do. What's great is I can answer all the questions but I don't have to perform all the tasks. I'm finding that acting is a thousand times more debilitating, because you're constantly trying to please someone. I find that kind of stress factor more difficult than the one of being asked a million questions and being the head banana.

When I was a young kid I figured out directing was the best thing to do. Making a film is a whole, collaborative effort but it's always the director who gets to choose from everyone else's ideas.

Her direction was detailed down to the underlying emotions of each character. She thought everything through from the point of view of all the players. 'Films are too important not to have a drawn road map. I won't wing it. When I come into a shot I always have an idea.'

Screenwriter Scott Frank, who had hoped to direct the film himself, assessed her skills as a Hollywood director along with her personality. 'There's no one in this town like her. She seems small and sad. You want to protect her. Then you find she's a pretty and intelligent woman who knows kick boxing. She's one of the few people who's not tongue-lashed in the business. This town is the biggest collection of dips, dopes and dunderheads.

Most are illiterate. Their entire vocabulary can be summed up in MTV. But Jodie's resourceful. She knows movies, but she knows more than movies. She's unpretentious – 99 per cent of the time she dresses in sweats. And she's maternal. She eats healthy and tells you how to eat.'

Jodie's simplistic approach to acting tended to make her impatient at times with actors who take themselves too seriously. 'I was much less patient with actors than everybody thought I would be. And to start with I was much too dictatorial. Luckily I nipped that tendency in the bud. I came to realize after a couple of days that different actors need different things. Being an actor myself, I don't treat acting with extreme reverence and can be quite brusque about what I want. But you have to give actors room to use their wonderful imagination – you have to let them fly. The same might go for other types of relationships, both in work and otherwise. A good lesson to learn,' she said.

One person who found her style much too dictatorial at first was actress Dianne Wiest and the two women clashed. Dianne requested a private meeting to thrash out their differences. 'The downside of it for me is that first-time directors tend to be very controlling which makes me feel suffocated. We had some tension there. But if I were directing my first film, I'd want to be very controlling too. In the end I was glad for some of her strong-mindedness.'

Jodie insists that she was fair-minded about everything and never held grudges. She would prefer people to meet her head-on. In fact she always welcomed debate and discussion.

I'm not a pain in the ass. I'm bossy but I'm not a pain. And anything I demand is always about the movie. It's not about comfort or vanity.

I don't like people that are afraid of me. It bugs me to have people who are obsequious. If someone's humouring or manipulative, I won't have it. The truth I can handle. I can't handle *not* knowing what they're thinking or feeling.

She acknowledged her tendency to be bossy by having the initials BLT (for Bossy Little Thing) embroidered on her crew jacket. She acquired that nickname from director Jonathan Kaplan on the set of *The Accused*. She makes no apologies for having strong opinions – they are what every director needs. Directors also need the strength of character to see their opinions through. Said Jodie:

You have to enjoy stress and pressure and you have to have a tremendously big and strong ego in order to do what directors do, which is, 'You may think that this is right, but I don't and it's my movie, so this is the way we are going to do it. We're going to make my mistakes and not yours.' I think you have to love being in that position where thirty-five people are asking twenty questions and you pick one.

If she was strong-willed and demanding, Jodie was nevertheless always considerate towards the actors, remembering occasions when she had been on the receiving end of a director's bad temper. 'Never make an actor feel like shit. It's happened to me more than once. No names.' Jodie does not want to be 'the director who says "You suck, you're ugly and you can't do a fucking thing." I think I've become the kind of director I always wanted to work for, someone you can make a complete fool of yourself in front of and feel safe doing so.'

One of Jodie's 'finds' on the film was Harry Connick Jnr, himself a former piano prodigy, who turns up as the male presence and fascinates Fred for a while. She was in the middle of shooting *The Silence of the Lambs* when she went to see Connick's show in Washington, DC. 'When I met him backstage he was, like, the most charming guy I'd ever met. And he has that southern, flirtatious, Don Juan-y thing. He really loves to perform for people. When we were trying to cast Eddie, I went through maybe fifty actors and I kept saying "Why don't we bring Harry in and see what he does?" Eventually he was in the movie and he was just great.'

The way the two males reacted both on and off the screen was just as fascinating for the novice director.

> When I saw how Harry was with Adam, how Adam laughed hysterically, then you know that it doesn't matter how much you feed him, clothe and take care of him, they want to be with some guy. They want their dad or their brother – they want some male figure. This guy walks in and suddenly he's not listening to anything I say. It paralleled everything that happens in the movie. For four days, Adam was totally in love with Harry Connick; Harry this, that, where's Harry, constantly. And then one day Harry was gone, and it was interesting to see that.

By this stage Jodie was thoroughly used to comparisons made with her own life, and the subject matter of single parenthood was an obvious one. At least it made a change from parallels drawn between John Hinckley and the obsessions of men like Travis Bickle in *Taxi Driver* or Hannibal Lecter in *The Silence of the Lambs*.

Jodie found herself expounding at length about her own childhood without a father:

> I didn't grow up with a father so I don't miss it. It's not a phenomenon that's in my psyche, it just isn't. I see my friends with their fathers and stuff and I just don't have that. My relationship with my mom definitely plays in how I perceive relationships in general. Single parents have to be everything – a policeman, sisters and brothers – and also the interesting thing with Dede and Fred is he comes to fill a place in her life she might have reserved for a guy.

She gives the example of one scene where Dede dances around the living room with her son.

You know if you had a husband around, you'd be dancing with him in the living room – you wouldn't be dancing with a seven-year-old kid. So there's a certain kind of romance that a single parent has with their child, and a certain kind of sisterliness. A kind of authoritarian thing and a kind of vulnerability that you don't have where there are two parents. It is a very peculiar phenomenon and I can't say that doesn't affect my dealings with Fred and Dede.

As she does occasionally, Jodie allowed one or two carefully selected journalists to interview her on set. Jonathan Van Meter, a contributing editor at *Vogue* magazine, was one. He was briefed beforehand by publicists, who told him he would only be allowed to observe her from a distance on set. But within ten minutes of arriving she was there in front of him, shaking his hand and inviting him to lunch. Whenever there was a break in shooting she would saunter over, light up a cigarette and continue the interview. Van Meter describes it as 'the martyr thing' – her overwhelming desire to be liked.

'Foster, who will talk a blue streak about anything – even, she admits, things she knows nothing about – often contradicts herself in her loquacity. One minute she's expounding on women's issues, sounding thoroughly feminist, the next she's saying things that would make Betty Friedan's teeth rattle,' he wrote. When he asked her if it was true that women had to wait until after they were thirty-five for the really interesting parts to come along, she almost took his breath away with her reply: 'The truth is that women aren't interesting before thirty. Men are kind of *born* people.'

While he was there he was fascinated to see her return a telephone call from a complete stranger, a student who wanted advice about taking time off from Yale. He had rung her and left a message and, rather taken with the cheek of the young man who tracked her down on a film set, she talked to him and told him what to do.

That she even bothers with calls from strangers says something about her stamina. She was and is a very fit person, and needed all her strength to play the dual role of actor and director. 'It is physically exhausting. You have to be on the set extra early for make-up and wardrobe – and then you find yourself directing others in a ridiculous outfit.' When it was over she said it was where she felt 'sanest and healthiest'.

> I found I'd just never been so happy. When I got back from a day on set, I'd cook soups and I'd watch the news and I'd actually read books. By the time it was finished I was tired but I could have gone on and done another movie three weeks later. I think it has a lot to do with being at the controls. Acting is all about being in the hands of someone else.

In the past Jodie was used to finishing shooting and saying goodbye to the film for about a year, when she was then required to do publicity. This time it was different. For the director, at this stage the work is only halfway through. There were photography shoots, marketing meetings, development talks and editing to be attended to. A trailer had to be made, and decisions about where and how the film should be launched.

Then Orion's financial troubles became overwhelming and Jodie had to go into battle to save her picture. Orion had funded its making, but millions more were needed to release and promote it and Jodie had to make the case for it herself. It is significant that *Little Man Tate* was one of the few Orion films released during the company's financial turmoil. 'In the course of doing that I started acting like a producer,' said Jodie. 'I realized I liked that.'

Having fought to get the film released, she had to wait to see if the public liked it. 'It's quite stressful, actually. The idea of now seeing your movie in terms of "Will couples go see it on a Saturday night?",' she said. If the film was not exactly a crowd-puller, it was well received by most of the critics as a good first attempt at directing. And it did make the profit Jodie had forecast – $25 million, having been made for under $10 million. One of the marketing ploys devised by Columbia Tristar Films UK was to show the film to audiences of gifted children and market the issue in much the same way as autism was marketed with Dustin Hoffman's *Rain Man.* 'When the film came out in America, people were only interested in it being Jodie Foster's first film,' said Jon Anderson, the advertising and publishing director for Columbia Tristar. 'The fact that it was about the problems of being gifted was almost ignored. We decided to market it.'

Some experts disliked the way the psychiatrist was portrayed as being totally devoid of emotions. Dr Joan Freeman, author of *Gifted Children Growing Up,* thought it was 'terrible'.

> It is a sort of Disneyland of what it is like to be a gifted child, and totally implausible. The child has apparently never played a piano but miraculously performs a recital of Mozart. The first time he gets on a horse he can gallop without falling off, and with no tuition he can answer mathematical questions that would baffle a computer.
>
> This is the image that I set about twenty-five years ago trying to break: the stereotypical view that gifted children are freak shows. Gifted and highly able children come in all shapes, sizes and personalities and they can be extremely popular and often have a superb sense of humour. This film will throw the issue back into the Dark Ages. It will give gifted children a very negative self-image.
>
> The ending may seem happy, but my guess is that the way the character is treated in the film, he could end up disturbed. He has a very low level of emotional reaction, no sense of humour and far too much pressure on him to succeed.

Jodie knew the movie was never going to be a blockbuster, but she was satisfied that it did well. It's a small film but it has a moving story and conveys with a certain charm and sensitivity the problems of fragmented modern home life. It was an honest film from that point of view, although it drew crticism from experts like Dr Freeman for being too stereotyped and unrealistic as far as gifted children are concerned.

It focuses on subtle events in the lives of its characters, like the boy and his mother dancing in the living room, the child's birthday invitations scattered by the wind in a playground, the birthday party to which nobody came – images of disappointment.

For Jodie it was a very personal experience to discover people's responses to *Tate*:

> I was on the back of a bus and heard someone say the film is just about two women and one of them is smart and one of them is stupid. The person she was speaking to said, 'How can you watch that?' I think I died a little bit. There are times in your life when that kind of criticism can get to you.
>
> But I learn from good criticism. It's interesting to see how people perceive things because so much of what you do is about how you communicate yourself. You want to do that communicating in the straightest path you possibly can.
>
> And if someone doesn't get it you have to listen and think about why they jumped to an entirely different conclusion. It means that there is something wrong with your performance or you're not really getting it out correctly.

As usual she talked a good argument, but this time she found she could not go home and forget about it. The film mattered to her far to much.

> I never thought I'd be a person who would go out there and worry if people would come or not. I pride myself on that. But now I find myself humiliatingly going to previews and saying, 'Do you like it? Tell your friends about it.' When you do something that is so much part of your life – I spent two and a half years on *Tate* – and every choice in the film is a personal choice, it has so much of your personal self in it.

Little Man Tate was certainly a labour of love for Jodie. She didn't want to start on another film as director immediately afterwards. Instead she wanted to be just an actress again and let somebody else take the strain.

> Acting is part of my personality. I don't think it's a strong part of my personality, but it's become such a part of my life that I don't

think I could do without it. But I love being a director. You're outside, you have to wear a coat, you have to wear a hat. It's windy and your eyes tear and you're sunburned. You feel like you're actually working. That's why I like dramas. They're really hard on you physically and they're very demanding. I guess I have a bad Protestant work ethic. I don't feel like I'm working unless I'm really working.

I do want to direct again but I think this was like a first love. It will never again be the same.

What's for sure is that Jodie poured her heart and soul into the entire process of making the film.

It's kind of the Everything-I-Believe-In movie. Orion was even concerned with my happy ending. I love it and I fought for it. The end has to be about the resolution of that conflict between head and heart. It's about creating a sort of misfit family that will have its own four walls, its own strengths and weaknesses. The foundation that brings these people together is that they are different and there's no place for them out there. I refused to say, 'If you're smart, you'll be unhappy but at least you'll have your mom.'

I mean, they spent years talking about the ending of *Thelma and Louise* – Susan Sarandon and Geena Davis sailing over a cliff in a convertible.

In Thelma and Louise's situation what would Jodie have done, she was asked.

'I woulda jumped,' was her unhesitating answer.

So from total control, Jodie switched right back into actress mode with a cameo role in Woody Allen's *Shadows and Fog*.

'I am craving acting again. There's something about performing that's unique and very intoxicating,' she said.

It was a modest part as one of the girls in a brothel in Allen's surrealistic vision of the twilight world of New York. Allen is one of Jodie's heroes, so much so that she had no idea of how the film began and ended. She was perfectly happy to do her bit and wait to see the rest at a cinema.

'I have no idea what it's about,' she said shortly after filming it. 'I just play in it – I haven't read the script. He has a different way of working and that was OK with me. It's his movie, it's in his head. There are very few directors that you trust so completely, but I do with him. It was his vision, so I did what he told me to do. I guess him and Scorsese I would trust completely.'

It was not like that with her next film, *Sommersby*, whose development Jodie had watched as it passed through the hands of Tom Cruise and director Sydney Pollack into Richard Gere's. When she first read the script the character of Laurel was a naïve and rather weepy woman who was duped by the impostor husband. Jodie couldn't bring herself to act the part of such a stupid woman and asked for a rewrite to make Laurel someone who deliberately chose to deceive herself. To get her on board, the producers went along with her demands.

After running her own show, she had to throttle back on her natural instinct to run everybody else's as well, but directors are well used to her by now. As *Sommersby*'s director, Jon Amiel, said: 'Jodie always has an opinion and will always share it. But she's disarmingly sweet about the fact that she's anal about detail and obsessive about timetables. She works with extreme intensity and by and large that's an asset.'

Sommersby was something new for Jodie. She was to play her first real romantic heroine. There would be love scenes like she had never attempted before with one of the film world's most attractive leading men – Richard Gere.

ELEVEN

Sex and the Single Jodie – Gay Protests

The subject of Jodie's sexuality comes up frequently in Hollywood when her name is mentioned. People inevitably asked 'Is she gay?' when they learned I was writing a book. The answer is that nobody knows, although the rumours are strong and won't go away.

In 1991 Jodie became one of several famous victims of a militant gay organization determined to 'out' stars who, they claimed, lived secret homosexual and lesbian lives. They plastered billboards across America's major cities with lurid posters branding their victims as homosexuals. The poster of Jodie read: 'Absolutely queer. Oscar winner. Yale graduate. Ex-Disney moppet. Dyke.'

It was a play on a well-publicized vodka ad.

Other stars who suffered included Tom Selleck and Whitney Houston, although Jodie's *Maverick* co-star Mel Gibson, married with six children, escaped. The poster of him was supposed to add authenticity to the campaign. It said: 'Absolutely straight. Movie star. Blue-eyed hunk. Married. Straight.' John Travolta, Kristy McNichol and director David Geffen were also targeted. Travolta and Houston publicly denied they were gay.

The organization responsible, called Outpost, which has no address or telephone number and is condemned by other gay organizations, received worldwide publicity and the stars were faced with the dilemma of either keeping silent or denying the slurs publicly and offending the homosexual community, at the same time attracting more unwelcome publicity. Nobody in Hollywood is willing to make an enemy of an increasingly powerful gay lobby, nicknamed the Velvet Mafia, whose members include well-known personalities, directors and money men.

Jodie was powerless against the outers. To take them to court, victims would have to prove that the reports were malicious. Outers deny malice, and a lengthy court case would simply keep the rumours going for much longer than waiting for them to die. The sheer viciousness of the campaign was a shock to Foster and the other stars named but they knew there was nothing they could do and their advisers told them to say nothing. Jodie's publicist at the time, Lisa Castellar, said: 'Outing is not something we want to comment on.'

In Jodie's case the gay campaign was relentless and persistent. Her silence seemed to provoke the militants even more, especially when the campaign met with some success and director David Geffen 'came out'. His admission that he sleeps with men seemed to do him no harm at all, and his power and wealth remained undiminished. But for actors and actresses who appear in heterosexual love scenes on screen it could be a disaster.

The rumours about Jodie surfaced again several times during her career. Gossip linked her with actress Kelly McGillis, her co-star on *The Accused*. There was talk of a jealous cat-fight involving another star, when the actresses had to be pulled apart by stunt men; but some people believe that this is one of those urban myths, like the one about baby alligators living in the sewers of New York after being flushed down lavatories when the craze for giving them as pets died. The story that the alligators grew into monsters has been disproved, but people still believe it.

Certainly Kelly McGillis appeared with a black eye which took a fortnight to heal. Fed up with the rumours, at one point Jodie broke her silence to deny them. 'There are always rumours. Kelly has since married. Nowadays people wonder which side of the fence you're on until you get married.'

The Accused director Jonathan Kaplan also denied the stories which emerged from the set. 'Whatever you heard, it's not true. It's so not true it's insulting.'

The urban myth is a phenomenon that has taken considerable hold in America and eventually filtered its way across the Atlantic. *National Enquirer* gossip editor Mike Walker believes he was one of the first to hear another such tale, involving a famous actor, a gerbil and homosexual practices. The actor is alleged to have had surgery to remove the gerbil from his rectum. Said Walker:

> There's nothing like these urban legends in the USA. They won't die because there are people in the USA who go in for mass faxing. That's how the gerbil story started. Somebody will write up something that sounds very convincing and they get a kick from seeing it take wings.
>
> I was one of the first two people to hear the gerbil story. We tried to track it down, with no success. I have talked to perfectly intelligent, sensible doctors who say things like, 'A colleague of mine was on duty the night he came into the hospital', so I ask him if we can speak to the colleague and it turns out he wasn't there at all, and so on.
>
> In this particular case the other editor who heard the story at the same time as me firmly believes it happened and I equally firmly believe it did not.
>
> With Jodie Foster it could be the same sort of thing. If you listen to the gay community in Hollywood they will tell you that everybody is gay.
>
> There is definitely a gay network in Hollywood, although I wouldn't go as far as to say they run the place. There are too many heterosexuals in the business. There are probably fewer gays in the business community than there are in the movie world. The difference is that if you are David Geffen or Barry Diller you have a lot of power. A minority group like that tend to stick together more cohesively than a heterosexual group.

Then there was the alleged gay marriage between the late Rock Hudson and Jim Nabors, who played the title role in the television sitcom *Gomer Pyle*, where his famous catchword was 'Golleeee'. Mike Walker explained:

That all started in the sixties with a couple of wealthy gays who would give a party every year and sent out wacky invitations with a different theme. One year they sent out invitations saying, 'You are cordially invited to attend the wedding of Rock Hudson with Jim Nabors.' At that time the idea that anybody was gay was unthinkable, but some people thought it was for real and suddenly it became part of lore. Journalists tried to run it down but never could. Yet it ruined Jim Nabors' career.

There were more gay protests over *The Silence of the Lambs* because serial killer Buffalo Bill is depicted as a homosexual, and once again activists called for Jodie Foster to 'come out of the closet'. Taking on sex crime as a topic for a film was risky at a time when the American tabloid newspapers were keenly trying to expose her. Reporters tried to stand the stories up, even staking out her home in the San Fernando Valley, but they got nowhere.

The *National Enquirer*, however, was not one of them. Said Mike Walker:

We have never outed anybody. We are absolutely against that. When Rock Hudson turned up with Doris Day looking like death we investigated it and found out that he had AIDS. People hadn't really heard of it then and it was a kind of education. In the course of telling the story of what was wrong with Hudson we had to reveal that he was gay and that's how he contracted the disease.

It was the same with Liberace. We wouldn't write a story about him simply because we knew he was gay, but when his lover sued him we did. We would never stake out Jodie Foster just to see if she was gay, although we might stake her out if we learned she was having a romance with someone famous.

Jodie Foster does not act like she is gay. She really is a mystery woman. She is probably the most successful star at keeping her private life private. It is much easier to write about Roseanne Barr, for example.

In the gay community, however, they consider Jodie Foster to be one of them, but she has never given the slightest hint.

Gay columnist Michaelangelo Signorile, writing in the national gay publication *Outweek*, said:

> Jodie Foster, time's up! If lesbianism is too sacred, too private, too infringing of your damned rights for you to discuss publicly, then the least you can do is refrain from making movies that insult this community.
>
> Is that too much to ask of you? You want to have your cake and eat it, too. No way, sister.

Clearly Jodie Foster has become a fantasy figure to lesbians, and the lesbian comedienne Lea De Laria alluded to that fantasy when she was interviewed in a gay giveaway paper. She was asked by the interviewer if there was anything else she would like to touch on and replied: 'Yes, Jodie Foster's vagina.' Mike Walker said: 'It's a kind of yearning among lesbians. You notice that she did not add "and believe me Jodie would love it".' Lea De Laria must be fairly plugged into the Hollywood gay network, and clearly she does not know if Foster is gay either.

When journalists interview Jodie they are warned that two subjects are off limits – John Hinckley and her personal life. They are told she will walk out if they try. Anyone who manages to summon up the courage to break through her steely reserve on the subject of her love life is met with reproof. 'Even to respond to that kind of journalism would be wrong,' she said to one writer. The conclusion, right or wrong, that many people have made as a result of this reticence is that there is something to hide. Even the most difficult of stars are seen with members of the opposite sex in a romantic situation at least once or twice in their lives. Not so Jodie.

Jodie's obsession with privacy has not helped to dissolve the rumours. When she is seen in public with a man it is usually an old friend or a fellow actor. There has hardly been a whiff of a romance, with either a male or a female lover. Her publicists tried to dream up an affair with British actor Julian Sands, whom she met while filming *Siesta* in Spain in 1987. Blond, blue-eyed Sands, one of a group of British actors currently causing a stir in Hollywood, accompanied her to the Oscars in 1989. Together, conspicuously holding hands – something that Jodie would only do in public for an obvious reason – they appeared at several post-awards parties. But Jodie's mother Brandy was with them and nobody was really fooled. Headlines like 'Jodie's a winner in love' appeared in newspapers and Jodie and Julian were said to be 'inseparable', but it was hardly a romance made in heaven and had more to do with Pat Kingsley's publicity office – her organization, PMK, handles them both.

Jodie's brother Buddy denies that she is gay, although it's fair to say that, as he left home when she was in her early teens, and seldom sees her now, he might not know. 'There have always been guys around. She sees a lot of guys. She just doesn't go where she's going to be seen. She hates all that stuff.'

Gay or straight, she is utterly discreet. She doesn't do the rounds of the celebrity circuit in Los Angeles. She is never spotted holding hands in dark corners of restaurants, and she often goes to receptions and film viewings on her own. She has mastered the art of moving around without attracting attention, and frequently travels to Europe without anybody realizing it is her. Whatever people may think, nobody knows for sure which way she swings, if at all. And one thing is certain. Jodie Foster is saying nothing.

At college her relationships were few. Her closest male friends were Jon Hutman, with whom she shared an apartment in her final year, and New Yorker Marco Pasanella. Hutman says their friendship was always platonic, although the relationship with Pasanella was romantic.

Serious commitment seems to frighten Jodie. At a time when most young women fall in and out of love regularly, Jodie was in the middle of a trauma which was not of her making. Her fear and anger took years to abate and used up her emotional energy, leaving little left for love. In interviews she has been noncommittal on the subject of marriage. She has a slightly jaundiced view of the myth of happily ever after, and has seen too many of her friends marry and divorce to want to risk it just for the sake of it.

Jodie has always been wary of the men who seek out her company because of her success. 'Hop-ons. That's what I call them.

When they see you're hot and successful they hop on your back for a free ride or at least an easy one. So far I've been able to keep them at arm's length. But it hasn't been easy,' she said.

In the brittle, thoughtless world of Hollywood Jodie's Yale degree and success as both actress and director scare many men away.

> My whole life has been filled with applause and very good projects. This is intimidating to most guys.
>
> I'm not one to be affected by what others expect of me. Like being a certain age, therefore you've got to find a man quick and get married because it's socially expected. I don't yearn to have a family but I'd like to have children one day when the time is right.

The 'airhead' mentality in Los Angeles has never appealed to her. As a child she was usually in the company of adults, and the stimulating years at Yale spoiled her for anything less than high-quality intelligence in men.

> For me to be interested in a man he has to have a lot going for him in the brain department. Aggressive men turn me off completely. I hate guys who feel that the only thing a woman wants is to be thrown into bed. This is insulting to women. The days when women were looked upon as a piece of meat are over. Men had better see the light of reality before it's too late.
>
> There is nothing more exciting than sitting down to have a damn good talk with a guy, exploring each other's mind and challenging ideas. To me this is just as exciting as having sex. So if I should meet a man who can deal with me as a modern woman with no hang-ups then the possibilities are endless.

Foster has a reserve about her that deters even the bravest questioners from asking her outright about her sex life. When confronted publicly she is deft at giving a dignified reply. When she won her second Oscar for *The Silence of the Lambs* in 1992, the militant gay organization Queer Nation mounted a campaign to 'out' several more stars including Foster. Spokesman Dean Tate said: 'We are going to drag every queer star out of the closet and into reality.' They chanted slogans outside the Dorothy Chandler Pavilion, and backstage she was asked about the protests.

'Protest is good, criticism is good, that's not against any American values, but anything else falls into the category of undignified,' she said, quickly diverting to the subject of her role in the film as a strike for feminism. 'It is very rare to see a movie where the woman is in the role of a prince who goes out to slay the dragon and goes through turmoil to do it and is better at the end. This is mythology that women are often not allowed to be a part of.'

Unfortunately for Foster, the gay mythology that she is part of continues to grow. Her only weapon against it is her dignified silence.

TWELVE

Into Her Thirties

Richard Gere doesn't even remember the first time he met Jodie Foster. It was actually at a dinner party at a friend's home in Hollywood, and he was far too interested in the four beautiful models also there to pay her much attention.

Their second meeting was on Oscars night 1987, the year before Jodie won her award for *The Accused*. They were at one of the many parties held that night in Los Angeles, where film-makers and actors who aren't involved in the awards pile around to somebody's house and watch the show on television. Gere and Foster were among five or six others on a bed in front of a large television, sipping wine, eating Indian food and watching *The Last Emperor* scoop nine Oscars.

Jodie remembers: 'Every time the movie won an Oscar he would lose it, ranting about how the Chinese did this and that to the Tibetans and how could they give awards to this movie knowing China's history. And I was saying, "Hey, it was a good movie!" We had these fights on the bed all night. So he remembered me that time.'

She was not the obvious choice to play the romantic lead opposite Gere in the remake of *The Return of Martin Guerre*, to be called *Sommersby* – in fact it seemed a distinctly odd pairing. The previous year, when Jodie went to pick up her second Oscar, militant lesbian groups outside the Dorothy Chandler Pavilion had chanted for her to 'come out of the closet' and forty-four-year-old Gere, then recently married to model Cindy Crawford, was also plagued with rumours questioning his sexuality.

Jodie, however, just turned thirty, had never felt so confident in her own ability.

> I've kind of gotten the big abstract goals out of the way. I'm in a calm period. Maybe it's the culmination of the number of years. What's the worst thing that can happen now? Maybe I'll get a bad review, have trouble getting a job – it's not such a big deal.
>
> I feel a lot calmer since I've turned thirty. I know where I'm heading now. I've got my tracks laid down. All that pressure of figuring out where I want to be and what I want to do is finished. I guess I just don't feel competitive with myself any more the way that I did in my early twenties.

Her mind was also turning towards the rest of her life, possibly even having a family. In interviews she would occasionally answer tentative queries on a subject that had previously been taboo. 'Yes, maybe I want a family of my own, sure, maybe even having a child – or not, and that would be OK too.' She has considered adopting a child, and has questioned her friend Michelle Pfeiffer at length about how she went about adopting her baby daughter.

When *Sommersby* was offered to her she was instantly intrigued, but not prepared to jump at it until they rewrote the script to make the heroine, Laurel, less wishy-washy and more of a woman who allows herself to be deceived by the man masquerading as her husband, Jack Sommersby, who returns at the end of the Civil War. 'I had reservations. I always do. I said, "This is what I want, get it there and I'll do the movie." The only thing I know I can't play is a weak, dizzy woman.' The first script required her to throw her arms around her knees and weep on the ground when she sees him for the first time. Jodie simply couldn't do that.

It pleased and even amused her that they did rewrite it for her, but this was not an actress throwing her weight around just for the sake of it. She simply has an overwhelming need to do things on her own terms. And it wasn't as if she had no other choices. She was offered the Demi Moore part in *A Few Good Men*, but turned it down in favour of *Sommersby*.

It was her first high-profile romantic drama, and although pre-release publicity billed it as 'hot and steamy' it was never that. British director Jon Amiel said he had planned a topless moment for Jodie beside a stream, 'but we didn't need it'.

Jodie plays a Tennessee farm woman whose indolent and abusive husband returns from the American Civil War vastly changed after seven years away. He has never been as loving and respectful towards her, and with the townspeople welcoming him home warmly Laurel must decide if she is to accept this man as her husband.

> This is a fully formed woman who chooses to embrace a poten-tially dangerous man. There are some beautifully crafted ideas in this movie. A component of love, I think, is self-deception and allowing the other person to deceive himself. Let's say you're married to a songwriter who's struggling to make it big. He thinks he's really talented and though you might think he's pretty good, you know, deep down, that he's not the greatest. Do you tell him, even if he asks and wants to know the truth? Of course not. And not just to spare your loved one a lot of grief – he'd be completely devastated – but by not bringing it up, you hang on to that ray of hope for yourself as well. This movie could be set in the present or the future – any time – and it would work.

Jodie was concerned that two people with a 'very contemporary aura' would spark on screen and seem out of place in a period drama. In fact the pair gave strong and moving performances – many critics thought it was Foster at her best, although the film did not make as big a mark on the box office as it was expected to. Off screen they were friendly, but there were no sparks either way.

> I can be high-strung. I talk really fast and make big gestures. I get adamant about things. And he is Mr Laid Back. When he gets nervous he slows down. We were like Laurel and Hardy.
> I like him a lot but really we had absolutely no drama off screen. He went off and read his paper. I went off and read mine. Some actors try and get something out of you all the time off

screen. You're always trying to avoid them. 'Oh, uh, I can't talk now, I've got a doctor's appointment!' Richard wasn't like that and I think our work was much purer that way.

Gere, who co-produced *Sommersby*, was mildly amused at having to play love scenes with the kid he has seen grow up on film. 'During our love scenes I had to smile. I always thought of Jodie when she was growing up as a tomboy. Her voice is not that feminine. It's strong and definite. And she certainly doesn't look like someone who might need help in a fight. But she sure forced me to bring the best out of myself,' he said.

When Jodie admired a necklace that Gere's now estranged wife Cindy Crawford was wearing, Cindy persuaded Richard to get one just like it for her.

Director Jon Amiel had heard how professional Jodie was on set, but was none the less impressed by the extent of her skills as a screen actress.

If God were to sit down and make the perfect acting machine he'd come up with someone very close to Jodie Foster. She can give you the whole third act of *The Three Sisters* in a single look.

She can be sitting, joking in French to the make-up man, with chewing gum and her glasses on. You say, 'Jodie, you're on,' and within thirty seconds she's in front of the camera, delivering a scene that will break your heart. Her experience as a child actor is what enables her to move in and out of character like that. As grown-ups we develop overlays, but Jodie combines all the technical facility of a child actor with the maturity of a really seasoned campaigner.

Reviews of Jodie's performance were excellent. The *New York Times* critic said: 'Jodie Foster has already won two Academy Awards but nothing to date is preparation for the romantic, resolute, elegant performance she gives in *Sommersby*. Ms Foster is so strong, so passionate and mysterious that she seems almost to be a new actress.'

And in London the reaction was scarcely less adulatory. Sheridan Morley described it as 'the best performance of the movie' and the *Evening Standard* critic wrote: 'As for Foster, words almost fail. Given her contemporaneousness, the modern idioms she has embraced most successfully and the baggage she brings to the film, her characterization is peerless.'

If *Sommersby* was a departure from her usual roles as strong working-class victims-turned-heroes, then *Maverick* was even more so. It was, she said, an opportunity to do something different, to do comedy. It could, perhaps, also have had something to do with the reported $5 million pay cheque, almost twice what she has earned for any other film. 'I'd been looking for a comedy for ten years, but I knew that drama is my strong suit and that I wasn't going to get involved in a comedy that wasn't quite there with people who didn't know what they were doing, because it's the hardest thing to do. And I never knew the steps you could take to make it better – whereas with drama I can say, let's fix this or that.'

She wasn't the first choice of director Richard Donner and *Maverick*'s star Mel Gibson. They wanted Meg Ryan, but she was too engrossed with her new baby and didn't want to leave home. Once again Jodie found herself reading for the role, and discovered to her delight that she has a real talent for comedy. 'I read it Thursday afternoon, said yes on Friday and had costume fittings on Saturday,' she said.

She had never even seen the original television series, starring James Garner, but fell in easily with the 'let's not take ourselves too seriously' atmosphere of the world of the laid-back card sharp. 'The truth about comedy is that it doesn't matter how it looks, it doesn't matter how it cuts, doesn't matter what they're wearing, doesn't matter if it makes sense. The only thing that matters is if there's a spark,' said Jodie, who was prepared to trust the experts in a field where she was a relative beginner. 'I'd never worked like this, but I've never been as happy and sane and unwhiny on a film before in my life. I just said, well, this is not what I do – I'm just going to do whatever you say. And I figure if I'm having a good time it'll be OK.'

Maverick's shooting schedule took her from the California desert to a paddle boat on the Columbia River, then out to the set of a western town in Arizona. James Garner, who has a cameo role in the film, starred with Jodie in one of her Disney films – *One Little Indian* in 1973 – and reckoned: 'She had a presence even then – such a little professional she could do whatever needed to be done. Her attitude and temperament haven't changed. She's just gotten better.'

As far as the rest of her life is concerned, it's getting better too. She likes to keep it simple and has recently been going through a pruning process at home, getting rid of the clutter in her life. 'I have, like, three cashmere sweaters and they're all black. Maybe I only need one. It feels so much better for me to get rid of things than to acquire.'

Although she owns a small two-bedroomed home in an undistinguished tree-lined road in the San Fernando Valley, she hasn't been living there for nearly a year. To be nearer her new suite of offices she is renting a house in West Hollywood. When she's not filming she drives herself to work in her black Saab station wagon. She also has an elderly black classic convertible VW in mint condition, which she loves. It has only done twenty-five thousand miles in spite of being twenty years old and she can't bear to part with it. 'My new car drives me crazy. It's a nice car, not fancy or anything, but when I first got in, I was so upset all the time worrying about it. If I went to a show or something, I'd sit there and worry that it was being broken into. Once I got a few dents in it I was OK. But every once in a while I drive my old Volkswagen. It makes me feel secure.'

Her taste in furniture is more high-tech than traditional. She's not fussed about having a home full of antiques and other valuable possessions, despite her mother's interest. The only thing she is passionate about is her collection of photographs taken by herself and various friends, for which she enjoys choosing fine wooden frames. One of her favourites is of a pair of grape-picker's swollen hands taken by an eastern European photographer in the 1940s.

She also spends money on pots and pans and gadgets for the kitchen.

I love my Calphalon pans, my beautiful ice bucket. I love those luxuries like linen sheets, bath soaps, lace pillowcases, really good smoked salmon, good Bordeaux, all of that.

I like beautiful objects, but I don't like the worry and responsibility that comes along with owning them. I'd rather die than have thirty paintings in my house that are all worth seven million dollars. So what I have are some cheap but beautiful photographs.

Although I wouldn't say I'm mean, let's just say I'm frugal. I certainly don't want to be dependent on making lots of money. I don't want to have the huge car and the yacht and the seven-zillion-dollar house in Beverly Hills with a huge mortgage so that I have to make films like *Towering Inferno* every other week just to make ends meet. I'd rather live more simply in the real world and have complete freedom about the sort of work I do.

Her brother Buddy described her as 'real plain wrap', meaning nothing fancy. 'As a brother I couldn't be prouder of her. She is self-made and very motivated. She is very sensitive. The things that are important to her aren't to do with money or lifestyle. She doesn't do drugs. She doesn't expect people to do things for her.'

When she's at home she does her own cleaning and cooking. She won't have anyone coming to the house – a legacy from her experience with John Hinckley. She is obsessive about privacy, and only her family and a handful of about ten close friends are invited to her home. She sees them regularly, and prides herself on having a sure instinct about whom she can trust.

During the months that she is not working she sets up a routine for herself, doing the same things every day, getting up at a certain time, making her calls, going to the gym and snatching her lunch sitting in the car listening to a tape. To Jodie a routine means control over her life, and that's what she likes.

It's always been my way of coping. I'd go to the gym, then I'd have lunch at a certain time. Then I'd go to this other place and have coffee and read scripts at a certain time. Then I'd go to the market. Not just once a week – I had to go every day. And then I'd make it home exactly in time for the news. The thing about being in control is it's a lot more fun than not being in control.

Her friend Jon Hutman says: 'Jodie is a planner. She has a one-week plan, a one-year plan and a five-year plan and none of them ever comes true, but she believes in them wholeheartedly at the time.'

For days on end, however, she will stick rigidly to her little routines. 'Somebody calls and says, "Come out and have lunch" and I say no, because between 12.30 p.m. and 2.30 p.m. I eat in my car. That's my thing, I eat in my car.' She has a telephone in her car. She hates to do business at home and doesn't like being contacted when she's on the set of a film, but her car is like a second office to her.

By way of quirkiness she has her superstitions. During the making of a film she will wear a particular piece of jewellery non-stop as a sort of talisman. On *Little Man Tate* it was a reversible pendant with portraits of Robert Kennedy and Martin Luther King. Before that it was Mardi Gras beads. When she travels she takes a special pillow along with her, not unlike a child's comfort blanket. 'It's not like I think it brings me luck. I just like it. I could sleep without it, but I always have it with me,' she said.

Her idea of indulging herself is to hang around at home dressed in her pyjamas, watching silly television shows and playing her favourite records, like anything by Miles Davis. She will watch old movies till late into the night and then sleep till 10 a.m.

She also loves to cook for her friends. 'My friends are very important to me. Some of them are in showbusiness, some are not. My friends are like family.' Whenever she can she will cook a huge meal for Thanksgiving and she's incredibly generous to her close friends, picking up the bill at restaurants and occasionally paying for holidays for both friends and family.

They are the only people who have her home phone number. Everyone else has either an office number or her answering service. Mail is delivered to a post office box number as a security precaution.

Some people love the idea that everybody knows where they live. I hate it. I've learned how to make myself healthy and how to keep myself from being incredibly anxiety-ridden.

There has never been a time that I haven't been in the public eye. At times I thought I wasn't but I was. And it's influenced my personality. You realize you can't be like everyone else.

Her personal fortune is estimated at around $30 million, but she still refuses to hire a personal assistant to do her shopping and all the time-consuming chores like posting letters. 'No matter how much money I make I'll always drop my own letters at the post office and pick up my own laundry. What am I going to do with my time if I don't do these things – make yet more phone calls? I'd rather live than sit there making phone calls.' She'll carry her dirty washing around with her in the back of her car until she gets a chance to pop in at her mother's house. Brandy has a washer-drier.

Reporters who interview her often come away with the feeling that, although she has talked non-stop and appears to be giving them a great deal of information, she actually reveals very little about herself. 'If you've been in the public eye as long as I have, your life is more important than the trivialization of your life to feed some curiosity machine,' she said. 'If you give people too much information, it comes back to haunt you. Hollywood can and will use every bit of information against you.'

Occasionally she feeds the hungry media a morsel of trivia which is so inconsequential as to be laughable, like the fact that she watches CNN for hours on end. Writers take it down and faithfully record it because it's all she's prepared to give them.

She feels her work should speak for her and tell the world all she wants it to know about her.

My work is my work. It has always been a way to express myself and to be the things I'm not. My character precedes my job. I was who I was before I became an actress. I became an actress because I like to act, not to get my picture in the paper and have people wonder what colour socks I wear – not to be able to get the best table at the Polo Lounge or to be good friends with Barry Diller.'

She doesn't hang out in the fashionable nightspots of Los Angeles. Nor does she go around, like Madonna, with a posse of minders surrounding her. The only vice she admits to is smoking, and there's a constant struggle to give it up. She likes a glass or two of wine but has not drunk to excess since her student days. When she goes for a meal it is more likely to be in little Japanese restaurants like Edo Sushi in Woodland Hills, where she frequently meets her mother for lunch when she's in town. She has her hair done locally too, and sees no reason why she shouldn't nip down to the nearest cinema and buy a ticket for a film like anyone else.

When she feels the urge she hops on a plane to Paris to visit her sister Lucinda and her nine-year-old niece Amanda, to whom she is very close. Said Brandy: 'All of a sudden she'll say "I just want to see Amanda" and Jodie is gone on a plane across the country, across the Atlantic. She will always go the distance for children. She has always been a care-taker since she was very small.'

In 1993 she dropped in on the set of *Mary Shelley's Franken-stein*, being filmed in England, to pay her respects to her friend Robert de Niro. She managed to slip in and out of the country without even being photographed. 'I've never accepted that there are things I can't do. It's really just the newcomers that think alienating yourself from life is the way to go.'

Despite the fact that she can talk the hind legs off a donkey – her conversation is peppered with the colloquialisms of a teenager on the one hand and the precision of an academic on the other – Jodie is a doer rather than a talker. She hates all the hype of Hollywood, the bull and the false promises of so many people in the industry who talk a good deal but don't deliver. 'There are too many people in this town today who know nothing about what movies are really about. To me making films is getting up at six in the morning and then going to work . . . and really work. Talking about it doesn't figure in my book. It doesn't really mean anything.'

She is simply not interested in half measures or people who aren't as professional in their approach as she is. She lives and breathes the business. 'Acting is indescribable. It's the thing that makes me upset. It makes me mad. It's what I eat. It's what I drink. There is really no way I could ever get out of the film industry. It's the only place that I really feel at home, be it as an actor or a director.'

As a director she feeds off her skills as an actress and vice versa. She's wise enough now to know her limitations and says:

> There are two things you eventually learn as an actor. The first is to feel you can do anything. The second is to know that you can't. What emerges is a balancing act between your creative side and your managerial side. One foot makes the choice of project, the other executes it. If you can only do one, you can't be a successful actor – or, for that matter, anything else.

It is almost impossible to separate Jodie the actress from Jodie the woman, because so much of her life has been lived on a film set. If one was to judge her from her choice of roles it seems as though at one time she was deliberately trying to work something out. She has played a gang-rape victim twice and the victim of a young man's obsession once, before moving on to what might be described as her 'hero' roles, in which she overcomes evil and wins through by her bravery.

Only as she entered her thirties did she appear to be heading off in a new direction with a role as a romantic heroine in *Sommersby*, a comedy Western, *Maverick*, and her latest production, *Nell*, in which she plays a strange young woman brought up in the backwoods. It is as if she has genuinely come to terms with the shadows of her past and is finally able to accept what she can't change and to grow. There's a new maturity about her both on and off the screen which bodes well for the future. She still may not think of herself as a big star or even act like one, but she certainly has an acute appreciation of her own worth and the ability to capitalize on it. 'It's not like I've had the most successful career in the world. I haven't. I've had a lot of ups and downs and movies that made no money and hard times and all of that. And I will continue to. That's an actor's life. That's everybody's life.'

Her growth as an actress has been steady since *The Accused*.

She admits that her work as a child was purely instinctive and she did not really take it seriously.

> When I was a kid, it was inferred to me that acting is not something you do when you grow up. It wasn't a profession for anyone who's intelligent. I think when I was fifteen to twenty, my acting was all about playing safe and looking down my nose at everything I saw. The truth is that I didn't give it enough credit, because when I work hard enough, acting is the most stimulating thing I've ever done. Performing is not something you can explain to someone. If you are a performer you can't stop performing.

If she has made a few rather average films she can at least say with conviction that she never made a film she did not believe in. Her choices have always mattered to her both as far as her career is concerned and in life. She does nothing by chance. She thinks deeply about everything she does. 'I used to endure anything to do a movie. Now I look at it as "Is it worth it to ruin my year by working with people I don't like or on something I don't strongly care about?"'

The constant merging of her screen life with her private life has made it difficult for her to form relationships. She says: 'The standard line I get from boyfriends is, "How can I trust you? You're an actor and you could be lying to me right now."' As to the possibility of her settling down with another person, she seems no nearer that now than she ever did.

She shows the same kind of quirky independence as a young Katharine Hepburn and one day, undoubtedly, Jodie Foster will be one of Hollywood's *grandes dames*. Hepburn has an unequalled four Academy Awards while other actresses with two Oscars, like Jodie, include Bette Davis, Luise Rainer, Vivien Leigh, Ingrid Bergman, Olivia de Havilland, Elizabeth Taylor, Glenda Jackson and Sally Field. Even in such exalted company, however, Foster is unique – only Taylor was a star as a child, and only Sally Field has experience as a director.

Jodie has always had a strong feeling of destiny and possesses enough self-confidence and courage to embrace it. 'I do feel I've been on a path that's been laid down for me. And I've always been absolutely willing to follow it. I always had this feeling that something big was going to happen to me.'

So why was she, among all her friends growing up in the movie capital of the world, the one who became a famous actress?

> I think it's something you're kind of born with. You know there are people who are very beautiful in real life, but they never look good in a picture. And then there are other people who can't help but take a good picture. I think I'm the latter. It may be something to do with confidence.
>
> It's not just being photogenic. It's more like instinct. It's instinct that tells you which way to put your body so that you'll look good. And I think I've always had it.

Jodie is very much a woman of the nineties, intelligent, glamorous, hard-working and attractive. She is not a one-dimensional Hollywood glamour-puss but an interesting mixture of super-confidence and insecurities. Yet she can be a bit of an intellectual snob. In interviews she talks non-stop, sometimes seemingly just for the sake of hearing her own voice.

Her sentences are peppered with words designed to impress, academic buzzwords and references to obscure authors and philosophers. Her friends say that she sometimes does it just to see how the person she is talking to will take it. She is testing them to see if they can trip her up or work it out that she's talking rubbish. It's also a trick to make an interviewer think they're really getting to the core of her personality. In fact, when they go through their copious notes, they usually find she has said very little about herself.

Clearly she does not feel the need to impress with showy possessions. She tries to keep her life simple and is not motivated by money.

> Most people say their greatest aspiration is being rich or famous or powerful, but I feel as though I had a good taste of that my

whole life. And I really don't care about that any more. I want to live an incredibly full life and my ambitions are more cultural than they are monetary. I want to have enough money so that I can go to any museum in the world, any restaurant, the movies, the theatre, so I can take out my American Express card and go to Greece. But that's it. I don't have any other kinds of ambitions.

Jodie Foster's story is an inspirational one. She is a role model for a generation of women who live life on their own terms, independent free spirits, answerable only to themselves. She is a woman who has conquered the Hollywood system without compromising her principles – a truly modern hero.

THIRTEEN

Egg Pictures – Her Own Boss

On the second floor of the prestigious Directors' Guild, an impressive circular smoked-glass building on Sunset Boulevard, Jodie Foster is having a Friday afternoon meeting with the staff of her production company – Egg Pictures. The suite of offices is tastefully decorated in creams and beiges and carpeted throughout in utilitarian beige, offset by richly patterned red rugs and cushions. An outer office where guests wait is simply furnished, with a comfortable cream sofa and a coffee table covered with glossy magazines. In one corner stands an antique birdcage with two brightly painted eggs hanging in it.

Jodie's own office is sparsely furnished with another cream sofa and a desk on which perches a Macintosh computer. The views from the window, overlooking a tree-lined avenue, are of West Hollywood. On the wall are a poster of the brown, yellow and black striped moth from *The Silence of the Lambs* and several black and white 'arty' photographs taken by friends. On a shelf is a framed photograph of a little girl peeking from behind a curtain – Jodie's niece Amanda, her sister Lucinda's daughter who lives near Paris.

Young and earnest-looking men and women bustle about, casually but smartly dressed, collecting faxes and answering ever-ringing telephones. Jodie pulls her chair into the middle of the room and they gather around her. Balancing a Filofax on one knee she ticks off items on a list, dividing phone messages into calls she should return, calls somebody else should return and calls nobody should return. She discusses the current position of about a dozen films her company is considering, finds out how writers are progressing with scripts, decides which ones need pushing and which need help, and which directors she needs to meet about new projects.

Her working clothes are simple but smart – black blazer over white tee-shirt and blue jeans – and her elegant tortoiseshell-framed glasses give her a businesslike air. She is indeed managing director of her own company, and perhaps the only actress in the business who could have convinced a film company like Polygram Filmed Entertainment to part with the $100 million it is likely to put into Egg's films over the next few years.

'The Hollywood community looks at her and they don't just see an actress. They see momentum,' said one studio executive.

Jodie is clear about her value to the industry.

> The truth is, one of the reasons I've survived as long as I have in the industry is that when people do business with me they know I'm going to show up on time, that when I say something I don't lie about it, that I can be trusted not to repeat something that's none of my business, that I'm never going to screw them and that I'll do the honourable thing. Of course it's hard to get to a place where you have the luxury of working on an ethical plane. I'm in the best position I can be in because I have a talent, a commodity I can sell.

Foster hatched her Egg while she was making *Sommersby*. Her previous relationship had been with Orion Pictures, who funded *Little Man Tate*, but when bankruptcy threatened the company Jodie looked around for another deal and found it with Polygram. The three-year agreement, announced in Los Angeles in October 1992, meant that Polygram will fund Egg Pictures to develop and produce projects under Jodie's creative directorship. Polygram president Michael Kuhn said: 'There is no doubt that Ms Foster is one of the most formidable talents working in the motion picture industry, with an international stature accorded to few.'

As she clinched the deal, Jodie said:

> I see this partnership as a unique and exciting opportunity to combine my experience within the studio system and my commit-

ment to an independent spirit in film-making. The idea here is to have more control over my own creative destiny and over that of the material I am engaged with. I strongly believe that alongside control comes a commitment to responsible film-making and responsible film-makers. Our goal is to build a home for both creative independence and sound financial discipline. I plan to spend every ounce of my energy building a production base that rewards both of those principles.

It surprised many hardened Hollywood film-makers that Jodie should even bother to set up her own company. She didn't need the hassle of administrating. She could do whatever she wanted without all the extra baggage. But she was determined to do it her way, as usual. Those who know her well understand that with Jodie it is all about control. And she needed something to fill the long days sitting on a film set waiting for the cameras to roll. With the aid of phones and fax machines she is in constant touch with her team of young people.

She chose the name Egg 'because it's feminine and about beginnings and doesn't sound like Greek mythology'. One of the reasons she set up the company is that she relishes the fight for better roles for women. 'You don't change the system living in Montana and raising horses. It's the responsibility of people in positions of power to work within the system and change it. You have to go for longevity. If you hang on, your phase will come back.' She was disgusted with the blatant sexiness of films like *Basic Instinct*, which she felt put women back twenty years into the era of being just sex objects. Those kinds of film were never for her.

In a world where appearances count for so much, Jodie is well aware that there comes a phase in an actress's life between the ages of forty and fifty when roles become scarce. After that they become 'characters', and Jodie intends to be in the business until she's sixty at the least. 'This is not a business that is kind to women, but it needs them. The female pioneers have to be ten times better than a man. Maybe some day there will be an old-girl network. But I'm not interested in alienating the audience. I believe in the system. I'm acutely conscious of the business in this town and how I organize my career.'

Sitting in a corner of her office couch, she seemed utterly at ease with her life.

> I have to say I've never been happier. In terms of the professional achievement stuff, thank God, I'm in a better place than I was. After the Oscars and directing I'm sure I'll find some new goals, but they won't be the big looming neon kind that can hang over your head. I would never want to be in my twenties again. I wouldn't have said so then, but I was very unhappy. The feeling of not knowing everything you don't know . . . it was awful.

As far as managing her company is concerned, Jodie draws on the principles of thrift instilled in her from an early age by her mother. Even as a child Jodie was always careful with money. As a family they didn't have the option of buying what they liked. Budgeting was a way of life. Jodie was encouraged to enrich her mind rather than her wardrobe and thought carefully about spending her hard-earned cash. Even while earning considerable money from movie-making she would happily accept a dollar an hour from her sister Connie for baby-sitting.

When she was fourteen her pocket money was increased from $1 to $10 and she always saved part of it, along with all her Christmas money. Once, she won a bicycle on a game show, sold it for $60 and banked the money.

'I like looking in the bank book and seeing the numbers have lots of zeros,' she said then.

By sixteen she was able to boast, 'I've got $2000 saved. In two years I'll have my own car, an Alfa Romeo. My mom gives me movie money and buys my clothes.'

Perhaps it was the fear of being without money that engendered her frugality. She still pares down her needs to the simplest requirements.

Brandy Foster was always very careful to invest her daughter's money wisely, although in the early days most of Buddy's and

Jodie's earnings went on living expenses. Jodie was lucky in many ways to belong to a generation which was protected from avaricious parents. She was smart enough as a teenager to want to know where her money was going. Nobody was going to rip her off. Most of it went into trust funds, which means that Jodie need never work again should she not feel like doing so. There was a time when she would occasionally say she might give it up, but not any more. She has come to a point in her life now where she knows she's in it for good.

Egg's co-chief of production Stuart Kleinman, thirty-eight, said: 'If you read old stories about her she would always say things like, "I could leave acting any time – I could always teach." But in the last few years I think she's entered a new phase of her life – she's looking at her career in the long term. And she's passionately, completely committed to the film business.'

Kleinman is a former entertainment lawyer who worked in New York, where his clients included Al Pacino and Spike Lee. Jodie's other key appointment was Julie Bergman, thirty-three, who shares equal status with Kleinman and whose background is in production. She said: 'The three of us function as equal partners. We each bring different talents to the table.'

At any one time there are a dozen or so projects at various stages of development. The aim is to make six films in three years – three costing around $25 million and three in the lower budget range of around $10 million. Jodie has the choice of whether or not she acts in them or directs them, both or neither. She also has the choice of distributor in a deal which is unique in Hollywood. A more usual type of production deal set up with prominent actresses gives the studios final say on the creative decisions. The Polygram deal with Jodie Foster gives her the power, with only a final veto in the unlikely event of her trying to put together a mega-budget film with no stars.

Finding the right scripts has been less easy than Jodie expected. *Variety* magazine buzzed with news of what was going to be Egg's 'first project', a co-production with *The Crying Game* team, with Neil Jordan as director. It was a story, still being developed, about an eighteenth-century villain called Jonathan Wild, who controlled gangs in London during the reign of George I. Jordan has a high regard for Jodie: 'To me, Jodie represents the best of what happens in Hollywood. She's been around for a long time – that's part of it – but she also never compromises herself. You can tell that just from the roles she takes.' The script has already been incubating for five years, along with another project close to Jodie's heart – the life story of actress Jean Seberg, which is being developed with Hexagon Films.

Stuart Kleinman emphasizes that Egg Pictures is not merely a vehicle to show off Jodie Foster's acting skills.

It is not a vanity production company to develop pictures for Jodie to act in. We're an alternative to the studio system. We want to work with film-makers of vision.

When we started talking about Egg, Jodie was voracious in wanting to know about the financial aspects of independent film distribution. Now she goes to meetings and executives are in awe of her. It's almost as if she was sitting there on the set with Alan Parker and Martin Scorsese and Adrian Lyne as a child, calmly watching and learning from their strengths and weaknesses and absorbing everything. She hates to hear this, but there's really nobody like her.

After two years of its existence Egg had in fact produced absolutely nothing until shooting finally began on *Nell*, the story of a young girl who grows up in the forest and has little human contact until a country doctor finds her and with the aid of a psychologist tries to guide her into modern society. Liam Neeson plays the doctor, Natasha Richardson the psychologist, while Jodie is Nell. Directed by Michael Apted (*Gorillas in the Mist*), with a screenplay by *Shadowlands* writer William Nicholson and Jodie co-producing with Renee Missel, *Nell* was filmed in the Carolinas in the summer of 1994. Jodie was understandably nervous about getting Egg's first baby off the ground. 'I'm really scared of this one. I think it's the hardest thing I'll ever do,' she said.

Unsurprisingly, she is totally committed.

I really believe Nell will be my most provocative, most challenging role to date. I suppose I was so attracted to the character because she's a part of me I've never explored before. She represents something, a secret nature we've all lost somewhere along the line.

She's this extraordinarily vulnerable innocent who doesn't know that when you're in pain you don't cry and who doesn't know you're supposed to be ashamed or that you're supposed to cover your body.

With hot stars like Richardson, Neeson (nominated for an Academy Award for *Schindler's List*) and Foster (herself a double Oscar winner), *Nell* had all the makings of a high quality film but it was an unusual choice of subject, self-indulgent in many respects and really only relevant in light of Foster's own subconscious search for a father figure.

To Nell, and perhaps to Jodie herself, Liam Neeson's character is the ideal – tall, handsome, kind and loving – someone who would protect her from the world. It is impossible not to compare Nell's experiences under the microscope of public interest and at the hands of a voracious press with Jodie's own.

The fact that she was able to put the money together and produce it, however, cements Jodie's reputation as possibly Hollywood's most powerful woman.

And if Egg fails? Unlikely perhaps, but it is something that Jodie has, of course, considered. Egg Pictures is very much *her* baby. 'If I fail I will have failed my way instead of failing someone else's way. I want to make my own mistakes – I don't want to make someone else's.'

She acknowledges the fact that at the age of thirty-two, with as many films under her belt, two Oscars and having directed a successful film, she is in a unique position in Hollywood. 'I forget how long I've been doing it, but sometimes it amazes me. Not too many people who have already worked for twenty-five years have as much energy as I do. Sometimes I can't believe how much I don't know, but sometimes I look around . . . and you know what I realize? I know a lot!'

EPILOGUE

Nell brought Jodie her fourth Oscar nomination, and pundits confidently predicted that she would carry off the top prize, equalling the great Katharine Hepburn's record of three Best Actress awards.

But the Academy Award instead went to Jessica Lange for her role in *Blue Sky*. Jodie had to be content with high praise for a superbly crafted film, even though it met with only limited success at the box office.

As well as the Oscar nomination, Jodie carried off a Golden Globe award for Best Actress despite the fact that she had originally been uncertain that she could pull off such a demanding role. 'I had to wait for a time and an age in my life when I was ready to be open. I wasn't even sure that I was ready to play it now'.

As had many of her roles, Nell marked a milestone in Jodie's personal development. She empathised with the strange young woman from the backwoods who was cut off from the world and shy about bonding with other people.

> The film was a real catharsis for me. I had never thought of myself as someone emotional. I'm not somebody who is effusive. I think of myself as more of a technician, and I've sometimes wondered if all this coping with life, people, stature, being public, keeps you from feeling.
>
> So I was thrilled, in some ways scared, to find that I'm not a technician, that I am an emotionally available person, and that it comes very naturally to me. It's just that in this world you can't be that way. It's too dangerous.
>
> Because people must survive, they will do whatever they have to do to survive. But every once in a while, you ask yourself what is it you've sacrificed. Being ashamed of being

emotional is unfortunately the by-product of living in a world
that is shark-infested.

Foster has become expert at swimming in shark-infested
waters. She causes ripples by charting her own course, con-
centrating on producing quality work, and retaining that isola-
tion that she recognised in the character of Nell.

In the hierarchy of Hollywood movers and shakers she is
among the top dozen. *Entertainment Weekly* has described her as
the most powerful woman in Hollywood. She is certainly her
own boss.

She views her current position with mixed feelings.

Everybody thinks the minute you enter into business as a
woman you suddenly turn into an ogre. But the great thing
about power is it gives you the ability to protect the creative
process. It's not about getting a better table at a restaurant.

The only reason I entered the business arena was to be able
to make films that were more vulnerable, to take more risks, to
do it without a bunch of fear thrown in.

What the power allows you to do is protect the work from
the system. And it makes my job much easier as an actor
because I can hire people I know work well.

Power also allowed Jodie to take her cast off to the wilds of
North Carolina for three months where they lived, virtually cut
off from civilisation. They lived in rustic cabins without phones,
television, or smart restaurants, and would cook for each other
after their day's filming.

It was an idyllic honeymoon period for the newly married
Natasha Richardson and Liam Neeson, and Jodie, too, revelled in
the simpler kind of life. 'I told my friends not to expect to hear
from me for a while and my office not to expect me to take care of
any business. I was really prepared to have a hard time.

'But the incredible thing is I never saw a happier crew. We
watched the sunrises and sunsets. We went on hikes and cooked
in our cabins together,' she said.

Increasingly Jodie is drawn to producing and directing rather than acting. She has recently directed a family comedy drama called *Home for the Holidays,* starring Holly Hunter and Anne Bancroft. She had no acting role in the film although she is now rated by *Hollywood Reporter* as the biggest female box-office draw, overtaking Julia Roberts and Demi Moore. Only Meg Ryan has equal pulling power for moviegoers.

Much as Jodie shuns the cult of stardom, those are the sort of ratings that bankroll her directing projects. Her name as an actress can make or break a movie.

During the summer of 1994, a $45 million film starring Jodie and Robert Redford was scrapped because the two stars had such strong and conflicting ideas about how it should be developed. The working title of the film was *Crisis in the Hot Zone,* and Twentieth Century–Fox had paid more than $350,000 for the original idea. Redford and Foster were signed up, with British director Ridley Scott at the helm.

Jodie, who would have earned $6 million from the film, had script approval and was looking forward to playing the part of Lieut. Col. Nancy Jaaz. Redford, who was being paid $7.5 million, also had script approval and wanted to turn the film into a masterpiece with an ecological message.

Time magazine said Redford hired screenwriter Richard Fridenberg to adapt the script focusing on his character. Jodie would have none of it, and another writer, Paul Attansio, was brought in to prepare a version which would keep both actors happy, but that was not enough to stop Foster from walking out. Such is Foster's power that as soon as she left, the smell of failure spelled doom for the film.

Redford decided to bow out because he reckoned the new script would not be ready in time. After a failed approach to Meryl Streep to take the Lieutenant Jaaz part, Fox ditched the project.

As ever, Jodie is finding that her power and fame is a double-edged sword. She guards her privacy as zealously as she always has, but she can't control everything. One particular thing is her brother Buddy, who, after years of languishing in his little sister's shadow, finally decided to cash in on her fame. He has written *Foster Child*, his version of their childhood years, and he hopes to have it published.

I am certain that Buddy's lengthy interviews with me prompted him to set down his story. We even talked about it over coffee at a shopping mall near his home. His frustrations with his own failed life as an actor were only too clear, and he battled against his feelings of loyalty to his sister and anger towards his mother.

The fact that he has written his book signifies to me that Buddy has given up the idea of ever being part of one big unhappy family again. He must have come to terms with his feelings towards his mother after all those years of analysis and realized that he is never going to love her or be the recipient of her affection in the way he has always hoped.

His 'dropout' years put too much space between him and Jodie. She is no longer the little sister who adored him. She's a very big star, and all he has left is to seek a kind of revenge— although he probably doesn't see it like that.

Both Jodie and Brandy are distraught at his betrayal, which laid bare family secrets they hoped would never be made public. Buddy had already told me much of the story. After Jodie learned he had spoken to me, I received a letter from her lawyers warning me of the perils of factual errors.

Buddy's book confirms the stories of a bizarre and turbulent childhood, brought up by a mother who hated men. He chronicles the incident when 'Aunt Jo' burst half-naked from a bedroom during a violent row between Brandy and her husband Lucius and put a gun to the head of Jodie's father. But he gives much more detail than my publisher's lawyers allowed me to.

'Then she laid down her weapon and embraced Mom, tenderly touching and kissing her on the lips,' says Buddy, who also remembers his mother screaming at him for bringing girlfriends to the house.

He says that Jodie was conceived after a particularly violent fight between his parents, during which plates were smashed. The fight was followed by a bout of passionate making up, but it did not save the marriage.

Buddy believes his sister Jodie is as bitter as he is about their difficult early years. She once told him: 'We have no family and never did'. That, more than anything else, will have prompted Buddy to spill the family beans. And doing so will have driven a final wedge between him and his famous sister.

The echoes of Jodie's early life can still be heard. Try as she might she can't seem to shake off the curse of Hinckley. She is the focus for a number of the nation's crackpots, some of whom now track her through the Superhighway of cyberspace. She has received death threats through the Internet, and although she steadfastly refuses to acknowledge them in any way, they cannot help but prey on her mind.

The Hollywood trade newspaper *Daily Variety* reported in December 1995 that Jodie had been targeted with death threats and other explicit messages on the Internet and that the FBI had been asked to investigate the threats which detailed plans for attacking and murdering her. The messages, which also described imaginary sexual encounters with Jodie, were posted in a 'chat room' operated by the Hollywood Network in Beverly Hills. The site's founder, Carlos de Abreu, shut down the chat room and sent copies of the material to the Los Angeles office of the Federal Bureau of Investigation.

It is Jodie's policy never to comment or respond to this sort of thing, and there was no exception this time. Although she refuses to allow these 'crazies' to wreck her life, she is careful about security and has never established regular routines in her life. She has perfected the art of moving around the world without drawing attention to herself, preferring to travel without fuss, and she will still jump on a plane to Paris to see her sister on a whim.

But she knows that the shadow of John Hinckley and people like him will never leave her.

The other ghost that haunts her is the recurring rumour of her

lesbianism. She refuses to comment on her friendship with her
Nell coproducer Renée Missel, but it is clearly a close one and they
wear matching bracelets. It was Renée who saw a Los Angeles
stage production of Mark Handley's *Idioglossia* and fell in love
with its lead character, the beautiful and mysterious Nell.

Missel acquired the movie rights and went to Jodie with the
project. Foster and Missel developed it together on a modest
budget of $32 million. As far as the world is concerned, the pair
are colleagues and friends. Foster will not comment further. 'I
don't talk about my private life and that's probably why I'm sane.
I knew better than to make the mistake of ever wanting my
private life to be public property,' she said.

Yet during one interview she talked at length about her 'lost
love' for a French seaman she met when she was fifteen years old.
She claimed, rather unbelievably, that she still wears the brand of
aftershave he wore to remind her of their time together. She also
said she had tried to trace him through French telephone books
and had sent countless letters to his parents' home but he has
never replied.

'He was in the military service when I met him at a New
Year's Eve party in Tahiti. I always wonder what happened to
him. Every once in a while I send a letter to his parents to
forward to him. It's been a funny thing—it's been so many years
since I knew him, but I can still remember absolutely every way
that he smiled,' she said.

This was an extraordinary admission from a woman who is
normally so ferociously secretive about her private feelings—so
utterly out of character as to be almost impossible to believe.

Jodie Foster, who never responds to salacious gossip about her
love life, is asking us to believe that she, a mature, intelligent,
thirty-two-year-old actress who has never been linked roman-
tically with a man for any length of time, is still pining for a sailor
she had a crush on when she was fifteen, even to the extent that
she still wears his aftershave. That's laughable.

Still, tabloids all over the world faithfully printed the quote,
which only added to Jodie's mystique. Nobody has so far man-

aged to track down the French heartthrob. Nor has he come forward to tell all about his love affair with one of the world's most desirable actresses. If he exists at all he may not even remember the effect he had on a skinny American kid all those years ago.

Question her too closely and she pulls the curtain down again, reminding you that she doesn't talk about her personal life. She will only talk in general terms: 'I've gotten more fragile as I have got older. I thought it would be the opposite. I thought I would get stronger,' she says.

She has, however, learned to cope with her feelings of insecurity. She even uses them to provoke a response in people: 'I realised that I didn't have to act like I knew everything was okay. It was a revelation because people didn't recoil in horror. By giving them a bit of power it helped me. I didn't get hateful or crazy either'.

Above all she has learned to trust her own instincts. She won Oscars for parts that people told her would amount to nothing. Yet she believed in them. 'What this teaches you is that you have to trust your instincts and that if you do what's right, no matter what anybody tells you, you'll have the best chance to be successful'.

Foster's instincts have so far stood her in good stead. She still has moments of self-doubt when she wonders why, for example, she never made it as a writer. But she knows her craft is filmmaking, and that will take her into the twenty-first century and guarantee the longevity she craved so many years ago.

In the end, you just have to get on with it, and that's what Foster does. 'You're standing there, you are in your camping gear with a big thermos in your hand, when somebody says they are ready for you and then you have to do it.

'It is like being an athlete. You can make decisions about how you are going to hit the hurdles, but ultimately there is only that one little moment of performance. You just do it or you don't. There is no way of explaining that really'.

FILMOGRAPHY

Feature Films

1972: *Napoleon and Samantha* – directed by Bernard McEveety. Nine-year-old Jodie made her film debut in this Disney family adventure. She and Johnny Whitaker are runaways on an exciting cross-country journey. Other co-stars included a lion called Major and a youthful Michael Douglas.

1972: *Kansas City Bomber* – directed by Jerrold Freedman. Jodie plays the daughter of a roller-derby queen (Raquel Welch).

1973: *Tom Sawyer* – directed by Don Taylor. Foster plays Becky and Johnny Whitaker Tom in a musical version of the Mark Twain classic. A song from the film, 'Love', was nominated for an Oscar and Jodie and Johnny sang it at the 1974 Academy Awards.

1973: *One Little Indian* – directed by Bernard McEveety. Jodie teams up with James Garner, with whom she acts twenty years later in *Maverick*.

1974: *Alice Doesn't Live Here Anymore* – directed by Martin Scorsese. Jodie is a tough tomboy who leads Ellen Burstyn's son into petty crime.

1975: *Echoes of Summer* – directed by Don Taylor.

1976: *Bugsy Malone* – directed by Alan Parker. Gangster movie with a cast of children, with Foster as Fat Sam's moll Tallulah, a speakeasy queen.

1976: *Taxi Driver* – directed by Martin Scorsese. Urban parable which won Jodie her first Oscar nomination, for Best Supporting Actress, as the child prostitute whom Robert de Niro decides to save.

1977: *Freaky Friday* – directed by Gary Nelson. One of those body-swap movies which worked only because of the skills of Barbara Harris as the mother who changes places for a day with her daughter, played by Jodie.

1977: *The Little Girl Who Lives Down The Lane* – directed by Nicholas Gessner. One of the best of her early films, in which she plays a teenage murderess who spikes Martin Sheen's tea with arsenic.

1977: *Candleshoe* – directed by Norman Tokar. Starring Helen Hayes and David Niven, it was the last of Jodie's Disney films. She plays a tough-nosed American urchin who masquerades as the heir to a fortune.

1977: *Moi, Fleur Bleue* (a.k.a. *Stop Calling Me Baby*), France – directed by Eric Le Hung.

1977: *Il Casotto* (a.k.a. *The Beach House*), Italy.

1980: *Carny* – directed by Robert Kaylor. Jodie is a bored waitress in a small town who runs off with the carnival and causes havoc in the hearts of two friends.

1980: *Foxes* – directed by Adrian Lyne. Four LA teenagers negotiate the tricky path from adolescence to adulthood.

1982: *O'Hara's Wife* – directed by William S. Bartman. Wimpy drama about a widower (Ed Asner) whose wife (Mariette Hartley) comes back as a ghost. Jodie plays the daughter.

1984: *The Blood of Others* – directed by Claude Chabrol. Adapted from a Simone de Beauvoir novel. Foster is a Second World War resistance heroine.

1984: *The Hotel New Hampshire* – directed by Tony Richardson. Jodie and Rob Lowe play brother and sister who end up in bed together, the least maladjusted members of a dysfunctional family.

1986: *Mesmerized* – directed by Michael Laughlin. Jodie is a repressed husband-killer in a true-crime film set in 1882 New Zealand.

1987: *Siesta* – directed by Mary Lambert. Jodie is an English airhead Sloane Ranger type who befriends Ellen Barkin during a weird holiday in Spain.

1988: *Five Corners* – directed by Tony Bill. A neighbourhood slice-of-life story based in the Bronx, with John Turturro frighteningly obsessed by Jodie – echoes of real life.

1988: *The Accused* – directed by Jonathan Kaplan. Brought Jodie her first Oscar as the girl who is gang raped and successfully prosecutes the bystanders with the aid of lawyer Kelly McGillis.

1988: *Stealing Home* – directed by Will Aldis. Jodie manages to teach baseball star Mark Harmon about the meaning of life, even though she spends most of the film dead in an urn.

1989: *Backtrack* – directed by Dennis Hopper (unreleased). Jodie plays murder witness who falls for the hit man.

1991: *The Silence of the Lambs* – directed by Jonathan Demme. A second Oscar winner for Jodie as FBI agent Clarice Starling who persuades serial killer Hannibal Lecter (Anthony Hopkins) to help her track down a killer who skins his victims.

1991: *Little Man Tate* – Jodie's first shot at directing. She plays Dede Tate, mother of child prodigy Fred. Also stars Dianne Wiest, who wants to take Fred off to college and give him a better life.

1992: *Shadows and Fog* – directed by Woody Allen. Jodie has a cameo role as one of a group of prostitutes, including Lily Tomlin and Kathy Bates, who discuss what men really want.

1993: *Sommersby* – directed by Jon Amiel. Remake of *The Return of Martin Guerre*, starring Richard Gere as the husband who comes home from the Civil War rather changed.

1994: *Maverick* – directed by Richard Donner. Film version of the old James Garner television series. Mel Gibson stars, with Garner in a cameo.

1994: *Nell* – directed by Michael Apted. About a girl brought up in the forest and the country doctor who introduces her into civilized society. Jodie plays Nell, with co-stars Liam Neeson and Natasha Richardson.

1995: *Home for the Holidays*

Director

1991: *Little Man Tate*

Producer

1988: *Mesmerized*

1991: *Little Man Tate* – with Peggy Rajski.

1994: *Nell* – co-produced with Renée Missel

1995: *Home for the Holidays* Paramount Pictures, with Peggy Rajski.

Television Series

1969: *Mayberry, RFD*
Gunsmoke (episodes in 1969, 1971 and 1972)
The Courtship of Eddie's Father (episodes in 1969, 1970 and 1971)

1969: *Julie*

1971: *My Three Sons*

1972: *Ironside*

1972: *Bonanza*

1972: *Ghost Story*

1972: *My Sister Hank*

1972: *The Paul Lynde Show*

1972–4: *The Amazing Chan and the Chan Clan* (animation)

1973: *The Partridge Family*

1973: *Kung Fu*

1973: *The New Adventures of Perry Mason*

1973: *Love Story*

1973: *Bob and Carol and Ted and Alice*

1974: *Paper Moon*

1975: *Medical Center*

Television Movies

1973: *Alexander* (after-school special)

1975: *The Secret Life of T. K. Dearing – directed by Harry Harris.*

Director, Television Special

1978: *Hands of Time* (BBC Series *Americans*)

Theatre

1980: *Getting Out* – directed by Tina Landau, Yale University.